Progression in Primary Design and Technology

Progression in Primary Design and Technology

Christine Bold

David Fulton Publishers
London

David Fulton Publishers Ltd
The Chiswick Centre, 414 Chiswick High Road, London W4 5TF

www.fultonpublishers.co.uk

First published in Great Britain by David Fulton Publishers 1999
Reprinted 2002

Note: The right of Christine Bold to be identified as the author of this work has been
asserted by her in accordance with the Copyright, Designs and Patents Act 1988.

Copyright © Christine Bold 1999

British Library Cataloguing in Publication Data
A catalogue record for this book is available from the British Library.

ISBN 1–85346–605–0

Typeset by Textype Typesetters, Cambridge
Printed in Great Britain by The Cromwell Press Ltd, Trowbridge, Wilts.

Contents

Photocopiable Activities

All activities are photocopiable and can be increased to A4 size simply by enlarging by 30%.

Preface

Progression in Primary Design and Technology is a book that places the issue of progression firmly into the classroom situation. It encourages the reader to explore practice and to develop a new perspective on progression for individual children. It is recognised that teachers have an extremely demanding role in which normative expectations and standards guide practice. Some children do not make expected progress for a variety of reasons.

The main purpose of this book is to provide activities through which teachers and trainees explore the issues and work towards classroom provision that is both challenging and flexible for all children. The focus on a limited number of mainly structured tasks and activities allows depth of thought and consideration of detail. Focusing in such a way provides an opportunity to reflect on meeting the needs of the individual within whole-class practice. There is no suggestion of a unique curriculum for each child, but that each child will take part in the whole-class experience as an individual. Design and technology provides highly relevant opportunities to develop and apply linguistic, numerical, scientific and information technology skills to a task. Thus, it enables progressive development within these elements of the curriculum too. Design and technology tasks provide an opportunity for children to demonstrate what they can do, and for the teacher to provide motivating challenges to develop the individual child's capability.

This book will provide some thought-provoking experiences enabling reflection on such practice. Practitioner research into their own classroom practice is recognised as being one of the most effective ways to improve knowledge and understanding of the learning situation. The activities form small-scale projects that enhance individual professional development. When several participants share findings they become relevant to whole-school development, and suggest ways forward that may be transferable to other school situations. The ultimate aim is to develop effective teaching strategies that reflect a higher quality of process for each child.

Christine Bold
Lancaster
November 1998

Acknowledgements

To my colleague Brenda Dixon for sharing her subject expertise and providing support and encouragement at all times. Also to my family for their patience.

Chapter 1

Introduction

Before reading this chapter, it will be useful for the reader to note their own definition of the term *progression* in relation to teaching and learning in design and technology. This will help to focus the mind and to explore whether the reader's understanding of it is the same as that of other people. This is not to suggest that there is a single meaning, but that there might be several ways of viewing the term *progression* and the way it is used.

As a classroom teacher and in my work with trainees on Initial Teacher Training (ITT), I have experienced working on a variety of activities that have focused my attention on the progressive development of capability in design and technology. A teacher's first priority is to ensure that children make progress. First explorations into what progression meant for individuals in my classes were through case studies and small classroom-based research projects in science, mathematics and literacy. When government initiatives established design and technology in the primary school curriculum, it was natural for me to turn my attention to the complex issue of progression inherent within the subject. The first challenge for the teacher is how to identify children's individual levels of development in different aspects of design and technology. The second challenge is to decide what classroom provision to make that enables progression to occur.

A good starting point in considering progression is to reflect on some aspects of the relationship of design and technology with other subjects in the school curriculum. Design and technology has developed as a primary school subject to the point where it is now part of every child's entitlement in a broad and balanced curriculum. It has strong links with science, in both content and process, particularly in the testing and use of materials and products. For primary school children technology also has strong links with mathematical and language development. A design-and-make task is a highly motivating and relevant context for children to learn about shape, space and measures – there is no better way to teach about different levels of accuracy in measurement for different purposes. Such tasks require a variety of modes of communication and may provide opportunities for children to write in a range of different genres. Engaging children in design-and-make activities encourages less confident writers to write up their findings and ideas. As part of the process, they recognise the need to be able to tell others about their project and to enable other children to learn from their experiences.

It is also important that children understand the relevance of historical developments that exemplify the technological process. The history of everyday technological products fascinates children. Looking at technological change conveys the essence of the design and technology process, and helps children to learn the meaning of 'meeting needs' and 'fitness for purpose'. Study of the historical development of the bicycle with children, trainees and teachers is an effective way of exemplifying the technological process.

There are also strong links with art, craft, Information and Communications Technology (ICT) and cross-curricular themes such as the environment. Each curriculum area has its own progression that should ideally be taken into account when planning design and technology activity and I shall endeavour to highlight some aspects within the text. However, the focus is the subject of design and technology; in order for it to maintain its own identity it is useful not to assume links with science. Scientific links in particular will receive little mention.

On entry to ITT, trainees may have a high level of skill in some aspects of the subject, perhaps having experienced technology at GCSE level, but often in one specific strand such as food technology or graphic design. Trainees often have a limited understanding of the whole process, as their own education seemed to focus on products. My experience in ITT includes the development of courses for trainees across the whole primary age range. This increased my interest in the strands of progression that emerged and became evident while teaching trainees how to recognise children's individual strengths and weaknesses. The aim was for trainees to recognise opportunities for developing children's capability in the subject, as this is an area of difficulty across the curriculum. Several years of teaching experience are often necessary for the skill of formative assessment at an individual level to become secure.

At school level, many teachers now have several years' experience in teaching design and technology. They have a sound understanding of the process skills and have developed expertise in the use of tools and a variety of materials. Despite this experience, there is concern about teachers' lack of subject knowledge and the Office for Standards in Education (OFSTED 1998) claim this is the main reason for pupils' lack of progress. In a recent attempt to improve standards of teaching in the subject, the Teacher Training Agency (TTA 1998a, b) have published texts to help teachers assess and improve their own knowledge. However, lack of subject knowledge among teachers is not the only issue that affects the standards of teaching and pupil performance in the subject. The greatest barrier to progress in the subject may be lack of suitable accommodation and resources to create appropriate activities and products. This has been recognised by OFSTED (1996).

Where they are available, classroom assistants often spend time with children completing practical design-and-make tasks, and therefore have a sound knowledge of the use of tools and the processes involved. They also have the opportunity to take courses designed to enhance their understanding of how children learn the core subjects and to provide them with professional qualifications. For all the above reasons, ITT and in-service courses need no longer focus on skill development alone. Courses designed to focus on the nature of progression and on how to help children develop capability in design and technology will benefit all concerned. Through such an approach, the skill development takes place within a contextual setting that encourages and stimulates deeper reflection on the deeper issues involved in progression.

OFSTED (1998) recognised significant improvements in the teaching and learning of design and technology but comment that the teachers' expectations were too low. Inspections identified that many teachers still did not use assessments to inform future planning and were unclear about differentiated work. This suggests a significant need for training teachers to focus on progression at a variety of levels. To understand what progression might mean for the individual child it is necessary to focus on the progression that actually exists within the subject itself. Looking at Key Stages is too broad an approach that fails to reveal adequately the progression that is so important. Much of the focus in current literature (e.g. National Association of Advisers and Inspectors in Design and Technology (NAAIDT) 1998) is on what children should be able to do at the end of a Key Stage, but provides few practical clues about how to reach the desired outcome. Consequently, children may not make the progress of which they are capable by identifying smaller steps of learning to use flexibly within the classroom. It is essential that progressive levels of challenge are identified within individual activities, and that design-and-make projects take account of small differences in the teacher's performance expectations. By identifying the small steps and becoming familiar with them, a teacher then gains the confidence to provide a slightly more difficult level of challenge for children as and when appropriate.

There is a need for teachers to be so confident in their subject knowledge to be able to 'think on their feet'. It is recommended (Design and Technology Association (DATA) 1996b) that a teacher build up a repertoire of familiar projects with different materials and processes. It may be preferable for a trainee to know three different design-and-make projects very well, and to understand the detailed progress within them, than to know ten projects in less detail. In identifying ways to help individual children progress, the detail is important and trainees usually find that their understanding of the progressive development inherent in a particular project grows each time they use it in the classroom. However, not all learners follow the same progression through a project and individual responses to a situation will provide information about how to modify teaching approaches.

For a variety of reasons, many children leave primary school without making significant progress in either designing or making. In a typical class of nine- to ten-year-olds, someone will be unable to use scissors well. Some children are unable to communicate their design ideas in high quality drawings by the end of Key Stage 2. One then questions what has happened during the child's schooling that has left them with a less than satisfactory competence in using a simple tool, or in using drawing to communicate design ideas. It may be argued that particular children are not 'good with their hands' or that children make progress at different rates. This is indisputable since it is widely believed that children have varying aptitudes for different aspects of the curriculum, through either heredity or experience.

It is also known that progress through most subjects, including design and technology, is not linear, but more often viewed as a spiral in which we continually revisit concepts at a different level. Nevertheless, a child's failure to perform at an expected level of competence usually indicates a failure in teaching, rather than arising inevitably from the child's own genetic inheritance. The teacher is in the prime position of control within the classroom and it is the provision a teacher makes for each child that holds the key to success or failure. Of course, funding levels determine the extent to which a teacher may make appropriate provision and the importance attached to the subject by the school. The provision of clear curriculum leadership, whole-school policy documents, schemes of work and in-service provision demonstrate the level of support available.

Using the activities

The aim of this book is to provide a professional development resource for individual or group use and the activities provided in each chapter work effectively with children, trainees or teachers on in-service courses. Exploring the issue of progression usually meets with a positive response because many teachers lack confidence in their ability to identify ways of enabling children's design and technology capabilities to progress. In schools, there is a heavy reliance on the long-term planning to provide the necessary progression. The purpose of this book is to encourage adults who work with children in educational settings to consider carefully the progress that individual children make in design and technology.

The assumption is that readers have a level of subject knowledge that allows them to understand the processes and techniques developed during the activities. The purpose of the activities is to develop and refine the ability to recognise specific needs and to cater for progression on an individual basis within the classroom setting. Activities are suitable for individual or group use. Some are specifically for teachers or trainees and others are for using with children. Some are useful at both levels. They have photocopiable sheets as a stimulus for group leaders to use in the best way to suit their purpose. The sheets will enlarge to A4 if required.

It is not the intention of this book to provide schemes of work or a host of ideas to implement straight into the classroom although there is an attempt to provide material within popular themes. The occasional suggested pupil worksheet is a stimulus for further development, but may be used directly with children if appropriate. The tasks are not generally open-ended design briefs. They are mostly focused tasks designed to explore specific processes as part of pedagogical development. Some of the activities may be joined together to form part of a larger project to facilitate looking at these issues through usual classroom practice. The aim is to develop practitioner expertise that enables reflection upon classroom events to take place and will subsequently inform planning for progression. The next three sections will attempt to clarify the nature of three important terms: continuity, progression and differentiation.

Continuity

Continuity and progression are terms often used in tandem. For example, all newly qualified and practising teachers ought to be able to 'ensure continuity and progression within the design and technology work of their own class and with the classes to and from which their pupils transfer' (DATA 1996a, p. 7). Subject specialists who are intending to become design and technology curriculum coordinators should also be able to 'set appropriately demanding and progressive expectations for individual pupils of all abilities within their classes which ensure continuity and demonstrate an understanding of what represents quality in pupils' design and technology work' (DATA 1996a, p. 7). Many experienced but non-specialist teachers should also be able to perform at this level. Continuity is not defined by DATA (1995b), except as it refers to continuity in learning across Key Stages 1 and 2, between each year, within a year and from Key Stage 2 into Key Stage 3. It is important to separate continuity and progression because they mean different things in an educational setting. Continuity refers to the provision of experiences and content. Ensuring continuity within a class is relatively easy, because the class teacher has a clear view of the experiences provided to children through the year.

However, all the strands that DATA (1995b) refers to are not as easy to maintain. A school may provide continuity by ensuring that all children experience the same type of classroom process when being taught design and technology. To achieve this, in-service training is required together with classroom support from the coordinator. Lack of continuity occurs when teachers have different expectations of their children's capabilities. For example, six-year-old children may have a teacher who expects them to complete annotated design drawings and to use them to inform making. The teacher of seven-year-old children may provide them with the design and expect all children to make exactly the same product. This is not the place to discuss the advantages or disadvantages of either approach, but merely to highlight the lack of continuity in the children's experience. In such a situation, there is limited opportunity for children to make progress in developing their own design ideas and skills in designing at age seven.

In relation to content, children may make exactly the same products in different years of their primary schooling. Expectations may be different as the child becomes older, but the danger is that the child perceives it to be the same experience, loses interest and therefore makes little progress. This approach is quite successful if managed carefully. For example, in a classroom that contains three different age groups the same project may be completed with different materials and clearly more challenging expectations for each year group. It is important for the school to ensure that there is continuity of experience. One experience can flow into another across the year groups, for example, by ensuring the children experience textiles more than once, with different textiles in different projects. Continuity is an essential ingredient for progression, which is why the two concepts link so easily. Continuity in both content and process will provide better opportunities for the teacher to focus on children making progress.

Progression

Capturing progression is no easy task because of the different strands within the subject. Figure 1.1 provides a model that may be useful to identify the relationships between strands of progression.

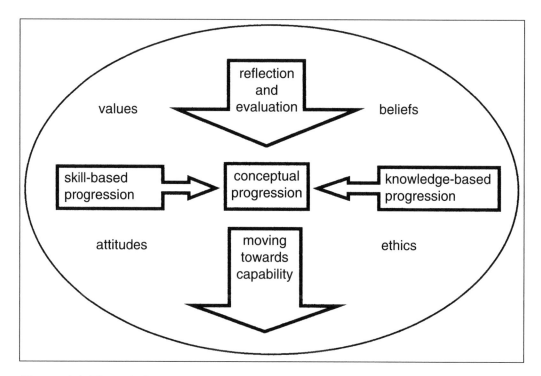

Figure 1.1 The relationships between different aspects of design and technology

The focus in some classrooms may be on a skill-based progression that teaches the children the 'know-how'. They learn to use tools for particular techniques and use these techniques in specific projects. In another classroom may be seen a knowledge-based progression or 'know about'. Children are given knowledge about different aspects of the subject, such as learning how particular mechanisms work, but may not apply that knowledge to design-and-make tasks. Ideally, children will develop design and technology capability through a conceptual progression that relies on applying skills and knowledge with understanding. To do this, children require the ability to reflect on and evaluate both the designing and making processes. They will also develop a set of attitudes, values and beliefs about the ethical issues involved. These will influence the design-and-make process and vice versa. The main problem for the teacher in planning for progression is maintaining the balance between teaching skills knowledge and understanding. The balance may depend upon the context of the design-and-make task, the age and capability of the children, and the materials used. In any one activity, teachers must plan for progression of ideas clearly based on all three strands.

Most children have awareness of design and of technology. They see and experience the effects of them in their environment. Many children have some level of competence in using technological devices such as mechanical and electrical toys. They can follow instructions and use tools. Some children develop a high level of capability in using technology to solve problems. They are able to identify the appropriate design skills and technology to use during the design-and-make process when challenged to meet a particular need. When working with children we can use their awareness to develop their competence and their capability – which is, after all, the ultimate aim. However, capability in design and technology is not attached to any particular stage of development. A six-year-old will demonstrate the capability expected of a six-year-old, and similarly a child of eleven will show capability at a level appropriate for an eleven-year-old. Deciding what to expect and considering how best to aid progress is the teacher's role. Progression in design and technology may be a process in which concepts are gradually explored in greater depth as a child matures (Kimbell *et al.* 1996).

Curriculum planners and developers often rely on their own experiences with children in order to place learning events in a progression. Decisions are made about whether a child will learn more effectively if one event comes before another (Hughes 1996). Hughes suggests that curriculum developers make assumptions about progression in learning which are unclear in legislative or planning documentation. As well as the teacher's own knowledge of children and past experiences with the subject we can also focus on what we consider the progressive steps within the subject, itself. For example, in design and technology, it might be considered necessary to make a simple two-dimensional framework before making a three-dimensional framework in wood. The third aspect of progression that Hughes (1996) suggests is knowledge of the process of children's learning. It is this last strand that focuses on the individual child's understanding of the subject. It enables us to reflect on why there is variation in performance and how the understanding of children may change over a period. The most important consideration is how particular teaching or learning experiences influence the changes in understanding.

Curricula are often constructed along linear lines, with activities moving from the simple to the more complex. A typical example of this is assuming that the concrete/verbal experiences must precede the written/symbolic (Munn 1996). Some educationists consider there is a fixed age at which particular skills ought to be developed. Munn found that the relationship between these two types of experience is much more complex and that the linear model is inappropriate for many children. An example of this in design and technology is assuming that under-fives cannot complete design drawings before making. The truth is that they can, when encouraged to do so through teacher modelling and verbal interaction. This suggests that there is a spiral relationship between the concrete/verbal experiences and the symbolic. Having the view that tasks become progressively more difficult as a child moves through the school system suggests that the progression is in the task and not in the development of the learner (Millar *et al.* 1996). A scheme of work embodies this type of progression. In this model of progression in design and technology, capability is viewed as moving from the 'novice' position to that of the 'expert'. It is very much a normative model, where children's expected development might be compared to what is expected to be the 'norm'.

Strands of such progression in design and technology capability are evident within current legislative documentation. The progression seems to be an adult conception of expectations rather than what a child may actually experience. At Key Stage 1, for example, children are expected to begin learning how to make structures more stable and capable of withstanding greater loads. Anyone who has worked with young children making structures will know that in the process of learning about these the children will experience a structure failing when loaded. Thus, they will learn how to reinforce the structure, though they may not master this skill until Key Stage 2. In this case, the progression is not linear, but a spiral in which children return to work on the same concepts in different contexts. Development in understanding structures is context-dependent. Working with construction kit components to make a tower, for example, is a very different experience to making a wooden framework for a model playground and yet they are both focusing on structures. To make progress in understanding structures it follows that a child requires a variety of experiences with a range of materials.

Children need to make progress in designing skills, in making skills and in their knowledge and understanding of a range of ideas:

- materials and components;
- mechanisms and control systems;
- existing products;
- quality;
- health and safety;
- vocabulary (Department for Education (DfE) 1995).

Capability develops through use of three fundamental activities and it is essential that the curriculum is a balance of all three for capability to develop:

1. design-and-make tasks in which children make products to meet needs, in a relevant context;
2. focused practical tasks teach children the necessary skills and knowledge;
3. opportunities to investigate, disassemble and evaluate products ensure that children learn about how products operate in relation to their purpose.

However, there is little guidance about how to use these different experiences to ensure progression.

Various publications (National Curriculum Council (NCC) 1990; DATA 1995a, b, 1996a, b; Schools Curriculum and Assessment Authority (SCAA) 1995a, b, c, 1996, 1997) provide sound, general guides to ideas of progression. However, many of the ideas presented are very general in nature and rely on the teacher to set the progression into contextual situations in the classroom. Indeed, some of the lines of progression suggested are not specific to the subject and are desirable within the whole of the school curriculum. In considering how to help children to make progress in their capability, the following lines of thought are suggested (DATA 1995b):

- pupils taking increased responsibility for their own learning;
- complexity of task undertaken;
- issues addressed in the designing and making, as well as attitudes and values explored and the levels of research, analysis and evaluation undertaken;

- movement to more open-ended tasks;
- range and depth of knowledge;
- application of skills and processes.

That progression in design and technology occurs through pupils taking increased responsibility for their own learning may be highly desirable, but it can also provide a false view of the process of design and technology. At all levels, the learner requires different levels of support for different tasks. Whenever a teacher presents a new design-and-make task, consideration of whether the learner needs focused tasks with specific tools and materials before completing the task is necessary. If progression is to occur, when a child is working independently then the teacher must be involved and must know how and when to intervene. Reliance on pupils taking increased responsibility for their learning may lead to the misconception that five-year-old children need a great deal of help while ten-year-old children require no help with their design-and-make tasks. Independence in learning begins before children enter school. During play, children guide their own learning, but suitable intervention from an adult may help some of the children's ideas to progress. In school, five-year-old children will take responsibility for their own learning when given activities that provide the correct amount of challenge. In contrast, ten-year-old children may require adult help when undertaking activities that are too challenging for their level of capability. Of course, even adult trainees require a lot of support and work less independently when using new materials and techniques.

The *Non-Statutory Guidance* (NCC 1990) is particularly useful in providing exemplary material following a skill strand through progression. Though this may be useful for whole-school planning, in many primary classrooms the process of planning for progression is not so simplistic. One of the items in the discussion of progression is 'pupils' awareness of their growing design and technology capability' (NCC 1990, p. C7). The pupils' own involvement in their development is crucial: a critical component of progression is realising that you cannot do something and accepting the challenge to learn how to do it (Kimbell *et al.* 1996). Children need awareness of their developing skill, and in practice, it is useful to ensure that they are aware of what they are expected to learn by completing a task. Children often have to undertake activities that seem to lack purpose for them, simply because they do not know what they are being expected to learn. Kimbell *et al.* (1996) also provide some very useful case study material to identify 'facets of performance' that exemplify issues for progression at each Key Stage. The facets identified are:

- investigating;
- planning;
- modelling and making;
- raising and tackling design issues;
- evaluating;
- extending knowledge and skills;
- communicating.

One aspect that seems ignored is that of the need to develop both breadth and depth of skills, knowledge and understanding with a range of materials (NAAIDT 1998). Chapter 4 includes further discussion of this issue and how schools may plan for the most effective use of materials to ensure progression in depth, at the expense of breadth, or vice versa. Much recent documentation focuses on the expectations at the end of each Key Stage. It provides aims without providing the detail of how to progress towards those aims. The view is of progression in broad bands of expectations at particular stages of education. In the classroom, it is important to look more closely than this and to focus on the means and conditions that enable progression to occur. It is important within a school to establish clearly planned lines of progression in process and content for the subject, within the contexts used to focus activities. It is useful to note that there is no set progression through a particular activity, although trends are identifiable. Progression in capability relates to the child's individual development. There may be general expectations at a particular age, but some children may well exceed all expectations at a very young age. Kimbell *et al.* (1996) observe that some young children operate procedurally in a remarkably capable way. It is their knowledge and understanding that impose limitations on their capability. We must be careful not to limit the children's progression by our own definitions of where they ought to be. There is no fixed linear route and some aspects require revisiting several times.

Many teachers perceive setting children tasks with an appropriate degree of challenge as extremely difficult. It is essential to understand the small steps of progression before being able to set the challenge at an appropriate level. More importantly, one must be able to respond quickly when the level of challenge turns out to be too high or too low for particular children. Kimbell *et al.* (1996) identify quality in particular process skills and then list advice about how to achieve progression. The suggestions made are all concerned with the detailed application of process skills:

- discussion;
- planning for economical use of time and resources;
- encouraging children to make decisions;
- the importance of the design as a working model;
- having a range of techniques to choose from;
- keeping a focus on the 'user' of the product.

They are all very sound ideas, but do not help the practitioner to understand the application of this way of working in the classroom. The idea of keeping a focus on the 'user' might operate differently with under-fives than with ten-year-old children. Under-fives making a model to take home might be more concerned about whether a parent *likes* their product, rather than about whether the product serves a particular purpose. One might expect older children to take a more objective approach to the purpose of the product, and to consider the environmental impact and wider social implications.

Past research demonstrated that children experience the subject of design and technology in different ways at each Key Stage. The lack of continuity of experience has implications for the progressive development of capability. The particular issues identified by researchers in classrooms across the four Key Stages were:

- autonomy;
- discussion and collaboration;
- the teaching of skills and knowledge.

However, there was generally progressive development in these issues across Key Stage 1 and Key Stage 2. The main difference lies in Key Stage 3, where the balance of expectation is different and the focus becomes more on the teaching of skills and knowledge and less on the process through autonomous problem-solving and discussion. This may have implications for the ways in which a teacher of ten-year-olds works. It points to the need for collaboration between the primary and secondary phases of education. More recent is the report that attainment at Key Stage 3 is improving as a result of the previous experiences at Key Stage 2 (OFSTED 1998). It is not within the scope of this book to deal with cross-phase issues such as this, but merely to indicate an area that warrants further exploration and discussion.

The notion of progression of individual design and technology capability is, therefore, quite difficult to define in terms of classroom practice. Ritchie (1995) also stated that supporting progressive learning for the individual during open-ended, design-and-make tasks is difficult. Research that focuses on following a group of children over a period of years to identify their progress is necessary. Much current research takes a cross-sectional sample that exemplifies general trends, rather than identifying specific lines of progress for specific individuals. It is useful to explore such cross-sectional samples and Activity 1 involves such a task. There is no expectation that every question can be answered accurately at this stage. The aim is to encourage the depth of thought necessary for reflective practice. The activity leads into a consideration of the need to differentiate for the child in future planning to ensure that progression occurs in one or more aspects identified. Further activities later in the book will refine this process.

Differentiation

Individual children do possess individual abilities. Most often, their abilities are linked to the experiences they have had, their personality and confidence in their own achievements. Children begin to make judgements about their own design and technology capabilities very early in their educational experiences, perhaps while at playgroup or nursery school. Young children will say 'I can't draw' or 'I can't cut', and one wonders what has happened to make them think such things. Children will often try to achieve in their drawing and making what they perceive to be an acceptable 'adult' standard. The experiences that make them think in this way may include the following.

- Adults often do the cutting and drawing for an item for taking home for a special event and the children perceive the adults' quality to be better than their own.
- Other children's products are better than theirs, particularly items made at home for competitions in school with parents providing help. In this case, the children perceive their own capabilities to be below that of their peers.

We should avoid presenting activities in such a way that children will develop this type of perception. It is better to teach the skills and processes needed for a particular task,

Teacher Activity 1 – Determining levels of capability

Aim: To identify a child's design and technology capability from available evidence.

Task: Gather *available* evidence of one child's capability in design and technology. The evidence might be of the design process, products, photographs, evaluations and class records.

Questions:

How does this child work through the design process?

Does the child evaluate with the 'user' as a focus?

What making skills has the child used?

What knowledge has the child demonstrated?

How does this child's understanding compare with that of other children in the class?

Reflection:

How can you help this child to make progress in developing skills, knowledge and understanding of the design-and-make process?

and to ensure that the activity is set at an appropriate level for the child. Provision made within the school day allows children to prepare for competitive activities with minimal adult 'help'.

It is inevitable that young children entering school will demonstrate different levels of competence with tools such as pencils, scissors and glue. One of the teacher competences listed by DATA (1996a) is the recognition of individual differences in children's ability to design-and-make and the related ability to respond appropriately to those differences. The difficulty that many of us have is the ability to respond appropriately. One of the problems lies in our own perceptions of how the child should perform the task. Our perception of performance based upon previous experiences with children of a similar age are sometimes set at too high or too low a level for some children. The most important starting point is the acceptance that children may vary greatly in skill level at any age.

Secondly, there is a need to recognise that this variance may result in children performing at a much higher level of capability than we expect them to. It is essential that there is early identification of children's skill level on entry to formal schooling to enable quality progression to take place. Young children in nursery settings produce designs that range from a single line on a piece of paper, representing a bridge, to a detailed drawing of an aeroplane including features such as windows. Some children may possess exceptional abilities that require nurturing in order to maintain individual progress.

At the DATA 1995 conference Iain McLeod-Brudenell (DATA 1995c) spoke about a child aged four who designed and made a party popper, using elastic bands and cardboard tubing, and then proceeded to peer-teach her friends! At five she designed and made a mask. When asked to record how she had made it, without prompting she drew an exploded diagram of it and later drew two other exploded animal masks that she thought people might like to make. This child showed exceptional ability for her age in thinking about both designing and making. Talented children must be recognised early to enable appropriate provision that ensures their progress. Other children will require different methods of teaching and experiences to enable them to express their ideas more clearly.

Differentiation means that adults first have to recognise the children's individual strengths and weaknesses. The impact of different teaching strategies upon different learning styles is important too. 'The challenge of differentiation therefore is to retain a balance between, on one hand, *respecting individual differences* and, on the other, holding a clear view about the essential qualities children need if they are to develop technological capability' (Kimbell *et al.* 1996). Activities must be planned that will enable the child to progress in all aspects, and the adults' role must be adapted to suit the needs of the children. For example, children showing exceptional ability in a particular project could be asked to peer-teach other children. This is not to take pressure off the teacher, but to help the child who is peer tutoring to firm up their ideas through instructing others, and to enable other children to learn from someone other than an adult. The act of teaching others enables 'metacognitive' reflection, i.e. children begin to analyse their own thoughts. Through this reflection, the child's ideas progress.

Care should be taken if using the approach that all children, at some point, have the opportunity to peer-teach, using their strengths and developing them further.

On the other hand, children showing poor skill development in a particular project may require sensitive intervention from an adult. This means providing the appropriate practical and oral support while ensuring that the children perform the task themselves. For example, if a child is having particular difficulty cutting a piece of wood with a saw, the adult may observe a difficulty in holding the wood still on the bench hook. All that is required is a piece of masking tape or a G-clamp to hold the wood and the bench hook in place. Taking over or asking another child to help inappropriately will not help the individual child to make progress in the skill of sawing.

Gender and differences in performance levels require consideration. The differences may not be apparent in all primary schools, especially schools where equality of opportunity exists in the ethos of the school. However, strong cultural, social and spiritual factors affect the way children view themselves in different situations, and the ways in which different gender roles manifest themselves. The following differences between boys and girls are sometimes evident in relation to design and technology:

- generally, girls do better than boys in the more reflective areas, such as identifying issues, empathising with users and evaluating products and systems;
- boys tend to do better in generating ideas and modelling them through to working solutions.

Girls also seem to perform better than boys when the task is loosely defined, the boys preferring a clearer structure. Theoretically, then, 'tightly defined and dominantly reflective' activities should not favour anyone. Nor should 'loosely defined dominantly active' activities (Assessment of Performance Unit (APU) 1991). The effects of gender are interrelated with the effects of 'ability' and contexts in which design-and-make activities are set. For example, girls might perform better than boys when the context is about people. Little is written about cultural effects on design and technology capability. All that can be said is that there are concerns about the lack of participation of particular cultural communities in science, mathematics and engineering courses beyond GCSE. However, it is possible that this is encompassed within a general concern that recruiting anyone to such undergraduate courses is difficult. There are no firm data about the effects of culture or religion in relation to the need to differentiate, but one must be aware of the need to consider such issues. In relation to the issue of progression the focus must be whether gender, cultural, social or religious differences have an effect on the rate of progression in particular aspects of the subject.

Before looking at progression for children, it is important that teachers reflect on their own current stage of development so that they too can move forward in their capabilities. The following activity is to provoke thought about your own expertise. This may have come from formal schooling, but equally it may have come from experiences in the home. For example, you may have learned how to create sewing patterns from a member of your family. When asked to reflect on your experiences as a learner you must remember that members of the family who taught you skills were your teachers, although you may not have experienced the subject of technology in

Teacher Activity 2 – Reflecting on practice

Aim: To reflect on your own experiences of design and technology.

Task: Complete the questionnaire.

(a) Identify your own expertise:
Qualifications:

Relevant hobbies and experiences:

In which aspects of design and technology do you have expertise?

What skill or knowledge development do you need?

(b) Consider your experience as a learner of design and technology:
What did teachers do that helped you to learn?

What did they do that was unhelpful?

Do you work best as an individual, in a pair or in a group?

Why do you like your preferred way of learning the subject?

(c) Your work with children:
Which aspects of teaching design and technology do you most enjoy?

Which do you find most difficult?

Give brief details of your most successful design-and-make task with children.

Why was it successful?

Give brief details of a design-and-make task that was less successful.

Give reasons why.

Keep your responses for later reflection.

formal schooling. Trainee teachers may have had little experience in actually teaching the subject, and it will be useful to gain such experience as soon as possible. It is also useful for trainees to discover the thoughts of teachers in their placement schools. This can help to provide an overview of practising teachers' thoughts on the subject. As a professional development exercise, all will benefit from sharing thoughts written in sections (b) and (c) of Teacher Activity 2 with others.

Chapter 2

Designing

What is designing?

Exploration of the design process begins with Activity 3, in which both teacher and children make a simple pop-up card. The simplest mechanism exists on template for a specific reason. It allows access at all levels while enabling a focus on progressive developments. The purpose is to provide a common activity through which the nature of designing skills becomes evident. The initial focus is on the aesthetic elements of design in relation to the mechanism provided.

Designing skills evident in the process may include one or more of these elements:

- discussion and gesture;
- using sources of information;
- drawing;
- mock-ups using scrap paper and temporary joins;
- trial and error;
- accurate measuring;
- planning a sequence of activities;
- evaluation.

The list is not exhaustive, but broadly representative of the main skills involved in developing a design proposal. No specific progression is suggested by the order, but it may be noted, for example, that young children make more use of 'trial and error' in judging size and proportion, while older children make more use of 'accurate measuring'. There is a clear link with mathematical development here. Of most interest is the influence of 'making' on the design process; the two are interrelated. Making the product inevitably influences the design process. In terms of progression, a holistic view is useful, but it may also be possible to identify elements that tend to precede others. However, one must never assume a linear progression, as any combination of the design processes is evident in a particular project. Indeed, in real-life design all elements are often present. For many primary school children the process will begin with making. This helps them learn about the materials before they begin to design with them (Johnsey 1997).

One must not assume that designing, as a specific phase of activity, has to precede

Teacher/Child Activity 3 – What is designing?

Aims: (a) to explore adult conceptions of designing;
(b) to explore children's ideas of designing;

Resources:

- activity paper templates photocopied to an appropriate size
- thin card
- coloured activity paper
- scrap paper
- measuring instruments
- various drawing implements
- scissors
- perforation cutters
- a variety of temporary and permanent adhesives.

Task:

Use the template provided to create a simple platform 'pop-up' card.
Decide (a) the recipient of the card, e.g. a child of seven;
(b) an occasion, e.g. a birthday.
Write a list of criteria that enables you to meet the required needs, e.g. indicate the number seven.

Design and make a pop-up card, using the paper template to provide the mechanism for the internal features and card to create the external features. Think carefully about any features added to the mechanism, taking size and shape into consideration.

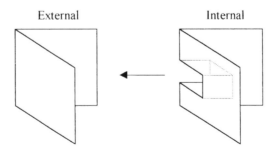
External   Internal

Reflection:

- How does the act of making a product influence the design process?
- Do all adults use the same skills?
- What reasons exist for any differences in approach?
- Do younger children use different skills from older children?
- Can you identify any elements of progression in designing skills?

A simple platform

Cut the solid lines, and fold the dotted lines to create a simple platform mechanism.

making. Knowledge of the materials and processes used in making is an essential element of becoming a good designer. Another essential skill is the application of previous knowledge in order to extend and develop a particular design. In simple terms, this is about knowing which processes will work in a particular situation. Designing, therefore, enhances 'conceptual progression' through developing thoughts, ideas and images about a product. Teacher/Child Activity 4 focuses on progressive development of the platform mechanism. Once children have used a simple platform mechanism, they may apply their understanding to design and make complex forms. The aim here is still to focus on the designing skills and to note whether the applied skills change as the task becomes more complex. The challenges become progressively more difficult. The purpose here is to consider how children can be challenged differently when doing the same task depending on their level of capability. As each challenge is completed, reflect on whether the approach to modelling changes with the level of difficulty.

Try the challenge approach with children. The challenges are adaptable to any age group, or one may wish to observe how successful the children are with these particular challenges. Children provided with plenty of scrap paper are willing to try anything when aware that they are modelling ideas rather than making final products. Focusing on the final product can lead to neglect of the design process (McCormick and Davidson 1996), while focusing on modelling through mock-ups will emphasise it. Focusing on the skills, knowledge and understanding necessary to becoming a good designer enables reflection on classroom approaches that provide progressive development for the individual child.

In real life, the designer sets the criteria needed to meet the client's needs. A clear example of this occurs when a person approaches a dress designer to create a gown for a particular social event. In creating such a gown, the designer will consider the status of the client, their personal attributes, the importance of the occasion and the impact upon others, including the media. An awareness of the impact of the design upon the environment is also important and this is particularly evident in planning applications, when refusal may occur because the proposed building is 'not in keeping with the locality'. Of most importance is the awareness of the values that the design portrays, but here we enter a complex arena, as 'values' is a concept that changes according to the situation and people involved. Design and technology in school provides a strong opportunity for the exploration of social and economic values and indeed such exploration ought to become part of the preparation for every design-and-make task. What is less easy to consider is the progressive development of such skills. Initially such values relate to the requirement to be prudent with resources, e.g. teaching children to cut pieces from the edge of a larger piece of card rather than the middle.

Children in school may also begin to make value judgements when they decide on the best material for the product. A simple example is badge making. A suitable badge to wear for one day is a reusable plastic wallet and pin that can hold a card label. Similarly, making products for other people, not only for themselves, puts children into a situation of considering what someone else will value in the product. Social values are thus considered. To look specifically at economic and social values a project that

Teacher/Child Activity 4 – Differentiating the level of challenge

Aims: To apply knowledge of the basic platform in creating forms that are more complex.
   To focus on the progression of designing skills.

Resources:

- coloured sugar paper
- isometric grid paper
- squared paper
- measuring instruments
- scissors
- thin card
- coloured activity paper
- perforation cutters
- various drawing implements.

Task:

Attempt each of the following 'challenges'. Each time you complete a challenge, write down the design process you followed.

Challenge 1

Use paper to model a pop-up mechanism with two platforms of two different heights.

Challenge 2

Use paper to model a platform within another platform.

Challenge 3

Create a 3D design using a series of platforms based on the mechanisms modelled in Challenges 1 and 2.

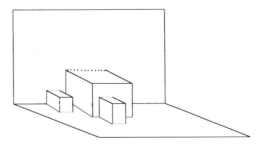

Reflection:

- Did your designing skills alter?
- What might be the reason for the changes?
- How can the challenge approach become part of classroom practice?

involves enterprise will focus upper primary children. As soon as children begin to cost out the production of their items and consider the sale value, potential market and possible profit, they begin to enter the arena of making realistic value judgements. A broad progression is evident in that very young children will mainly be able to focus on their own preferences, but be given encouragement to focus on the wider school issues. Older children will gradually become more aware of the needs of the customer, and the implications of economic and social values for the quality of product.

Another issue that arises in schools is whether children design as individuals, in groups or as part of a team and how different organisational strategies may lead to the development of different skills, knowledge and understanding. Designing in a group situation is the most problematic. A group situation implies cooperation and collaboration to make the same product. Children having vastly different visions of the outcome may outweigh the benefit of working together on a collaborative venture. The result may be a high level of discord, leaving children feeling undervalued, as other ideas are favoured. The key to success is the teacher's management of the situation, and recognition that one cannot impose adult expectations of cooperation onto children. Put into a situation of designing as a group of four, children will often split into two teams, or even decide that the one with the better drawing skills becomes the designer. This then becomes a team, rather than a group, in which one child is the designer and other roles belong to the rest. One child may make progress with designing skills while the others do not. If this becomes a preferred way of working then the teacher must be proactive to ensure that over a period all children accept the role of designer in turn. Alternatively, the original group may require the development of a broader concept of designing, and be encouraged to use brainstorming and other techniques to focus their attention on collaborative approaches to designing.

When children work in pairs or larger groups one must consider development of individual skill, knowledge and understanding. Groups of three or more are rarely successful with many primary school children. Working as a team, carefully orchestrated by the teacher, may overcome problems and ensure effective learning through cooperation. Ideally, all members of the team will contribute to both the designing and the making of the whole product, but may be involved in different parts of the project. For example, creating a pets' playground (Child Activity 6) lends itself to children designing and making a small part that has to fit into the whole structure. One child may be responsible for the ladder, another for the slide, and yet another for the supporting framework.

Cognitive modelling

Cognitive modelling is the process that occurs internally and relies on being able to link the external sensory inputs with previous knowledge. It is a process by which a person visualises what the outcome will be, depending on materials used and processes followed. Designing is an interaction between mind and hand, as illustrated in the APU model (1991). The model suggests that designers begin with 'hazy impressions' in the mind that then confront reality and pass through an interactive process of concrete and cognitive modelling. Although the model provides for progressive development of the designing process, it does not provide a model for teaching and learning the process. Very young children often have very definite ideas about what they wish to make, and are unused to having 'hazy ideas' that they modify and refine. In school there is often emphasis on the concrete modelling, when children are expected to produce a design drawing or to model ideas with other materials before making. In reality, the balance between cognitive modelling and concrete modelling will depend on the materials used. Murray (1994) suggests that when working with food much of the designing occurs as cognitive modelling.

A chef may decide that adding a particular spice to a recipe or changing the quantities will create a different flavour. Decisions rely on the chef's knowledge of the ingredients. The chef knows whether they combine well to create particular effects. The 'model' is then subject to evaluation and modification. Drawing is an unnecessary element in creating a new dish, but writing down the recipe (equivalent to a plan in other contexts) is crucial to enable replication. Teaching approaches that enable the progressive development of both cognitive and concrete modelling are necessary. Each is crucial to the development of the other.

Brainstorming

Brainstorming occurs in a solitary or group situation. The teacher or the children may take control of the situation. It is a particularly useful technique for encouraging young

Figure 2.1 Chef's choice

children to reflect on their current ideas and to share them with others. Being able to remember and imagine something you have seen, and then to reproduce it on paper or in a model, is a sophisticated process (Johnsey 1994). Brainstorming helps children to share this process and develop each other's ideas. A successful use of this approach was outlined by Iain McLeod-Brudenell (DATA 1995c). Children in a nursery contributed various ideas about the construction of a house. The teacher compiled the suggestions on a large sheet and although the children were unable to read them, they knew the exact place of their own idea. Some children showed understanding of systems, such as the electricity system and water system. There was recognition that the wires and pipes were mostly hidden and that they only worked under a person's control. The subsequent construction that all children contributed to included items to represent these systems. In contrast, asking children to make a house without previous brainstorming may lead to a more aesthetically oriented outcome as the child focuses on external rather than internal features. Thus, the brainstorming enables the children to articulate their cognitive models then translate them into practice. Older children may brainstorm in their peer groups, thus enabling an exchange of perspectives and insights that is essential to a collaborative design process (Dunn and Larson 1990).

A similar approach is useful when creating a role-play area. Children are often used to making dens, and have various ideas about different types of buildings designed for different purposes. By articulating ideas, the children begin to use cognitive modelling in making decisions about where to place items in the role-play area. The children pass through the whole design-and-make process. Of course, in whole-class situations individual development is more difficult to identify and so the recommendation is for variety in class grouping. The benefit is that the teacher models the approach so children may then use the same approach more independently later on.

Creating a role-play area with the children also emphasises the importance of planning as part of the process. Evaluation becomes an integral part of the process as the children begin to think about the best layout for items in the area. The children have to visualise the area, use trial and error, and will enter a process of continual evaluation and redesign. Of course, children who have limited previous experience of a particular environment, such as a hospital, will have more difficulty visualising than will children with experience. The whole process requires real-life experience and visits to appropriate places to enable the children to create cognitive models. On such a visit observational drawings, photographs and videos aid the design process.

Modelling through drawing

Teacher Activity 5 explores preferred drawing styles. It is important for teachers to be aware of their own strengths and weaknesses in this area and to be aware of the range of styles and techniques to teach the children. Practice is the key to confidence and success. Let the children see you drawing, and practising different techniques. Ensure that a range of graphic media is available.

The activity demonstrates that people use different skills and that specific types of design drawings are suited to particular purposes. For example, a builder usually works

Teacher Activity 5 – Redesigning the staff room

Aim: To explore preferred drawing techniques and consider possibilities for progressive development of such skills, in relation to identifying and meeting needs.

Resources:

- plain paper, A4–A2 sizes available
- squared paper, A4–A2 sizes available
- drawing pencils
- measuring instruments
- isometric paper.

Individual task:

As part of the school improvement plan, the staff room needs redesigning. The contractors are keen to involve the staff in deciding on the improvements and have consulted with you. You have decided to produce design drawings to illustrate more clearly what you would like your staff room to be like.

First, after discussion with colleagues, make a list of everyone's needs. Consider yourselves, parents and other visitors. Economic and social factors are also important considerations.

Second – *using any drawing techniques that you feel comfortable with* – develop individual drawings that include the desired features.

Group reflection:

- Discuss the merits of the different approaches.
- Which drawings are best for the builder to use? Why?

- Which are best for the interior designer? Why?

- What skill development do you need to enable you to provide appropriate design challenges within the classroom situation?

from plans with an aerial view and side elevations having accurate measurements. The question the activity may raise is whether a particular style of design drawing is more difficult, and whether there is a progression in the development of such skills.

The following lists may suggest a progressive development:

• observational drawing	drawing in two dimensions
• annotated diagrams	drawing in three dimensions
• exploded diagrams	
• technical drawing	
• drawing to scale	
• aerial views and side elevations	
• floor plans and cross-sections	
• isometric drawing	
• perspective drawing.	

Drawing in different dimensions will occur in the other types earlier in the list, i.e. observational drawing may be two- or three-dimensional. Generally, two-dimensional drawing will occur before three-dimensional skills are developed. Representing a three-dimensional product on a two-dimensional plane requires sophisticated perceptual skills that many primary school children take a long time to develop. Conversely, special types of two-dimensional drawings such as plans create their own difficulties for children as discussed later. Teachers often expect children to acquire the sophisticated skill of designing in two dimensions a three-dimensional product, without reflection on the necessary conceptual development. The result is often a picture of a product rather than a working design (Constable 1994b). The intellectual demands of asking children to visualise a three-dimensional product in two-dimensional form are enormous. All the complexities of perspective and scale begin to overlap (Anning 1993). To help them overcome the difficulties children need to learn about the different drawing conventions and skills for different purposes.

The list is not exhaustive, but provides a broad outline of styles. However, it does not necessarily reflect a distinct progression, although there may be certain trends. Young children tend to draw from their imagination, based on pictures or actual objects they have seen. They will draw the features that 'catch their eye' as important to them. This may be the shape of an arched bridge, or the number of square windows on a building. This may be the beginnings of observational drawing, but not truly observational in the sense that they have not focused on specific aspects of the design with a view to making a product. For observational drawing to be purposeful, teacher support, questioning and guidance will help the child identify the salient features in more detail. A simple example is noticing that all window frames have width and therefore a single pencil line is insufficient. Observational freehand drawing is a technique to refine and develop at all levels, and is often the starting point for a design project. Some very young children may be able to draw sectional drawings without consciously being aware that they are doing so. For example, a five-year-old on a boat trip, sitting on the lower deck, drew a sectional drawing of the boat freehand. The detail included the seats and the people sitting on them. It emerged purely from the child's observation of the situation.

A range of graphic media is available in most primary schools and fully utilised in the development of design ideas. Freehand drawing skills using pencil ought to be encouraged throughout primary school and beyond. Children need to learn the techniques of how to use a pencil to create straight lines, curved lines and shading effects (Scrine and Clewes 1989). They must become confident in their skills and not afraid to make tentative marks on paper to allow modification and change. Drawing from different points of view aids development of links between two and three dimensions. Children become aware of the effect their product will have in a more holistic way. Child Activity 6 involves observation of children drawing small objects from different points of view.

Working with small objects on the desktop allows the child the opportunity to position the object and themselves to look at a variety of views very easily. Elevations

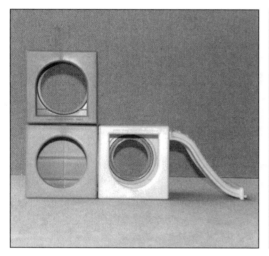

Figure 2.2 Side view of a hamster climbing frame

Figure 2.3 Top view of a hamster climbing frame

Figure 2.4 Front view of a hamster climbing frame

Child Activity 6 – Different points of view

Aim: To observe the ways in which children illustrate three-dimensional objects in two-dimensional form, and to consider ways in which to enable progression.

Resources:

- a selection of pet 'toys'
- drawing paper
- drawing pencils
- drawing boards.

Task:

The school hamster is in need of a new playground. Before making the playground the children evaluate existing products. Encourage the children to observe the products from different points of view. They must note the merits of each item and consider the suitability of specific features, e.g. the space between the rungs of a ladder. The children will sketch any features that they wish to include in their own playground design. They will sketch the same features from different viewpoints, e.g. a ladder may be sketched from the front and from the side.

A pet's playground 1

1. Look carefully at the pet toys.

2. Decide which items you will include in your playground design.

3. Sketch those items from two or three different viewpoints, e.g.:

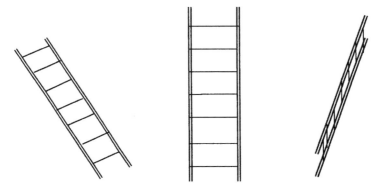

4. Think about how you will include these ideas in your final design.

and plan views are useful and experience of these translates easily into orthographic projections later. Oblique views are also useful, as are considerations of what the object would look like if sawn in cross-section. Children also require experience in three-dimensional drawing, and must eventually learn techniques to aid the development of perspective. However, too much early emphasis on technical drawing with accurate measurements can stifle the skill development of freehand drawing. The drawing is not a product in itself but part of a process. In this sense, the initial quality of the drawing is not as important as the development of skills of observation. Children should also become aware that several drawings might clarify ideas and try out different effects. All drawings from initial tentative sketches to final designs ought to be valued by keeping a portfolio that also includes evaluative records as part of the process. Such a portfolio is a valuable contribution to developing capability (Bratt and Djora 1995).

From nursery, children may be encouraged to observe and draw from different perspectives. Under-fives benefit from adult modelling and intervention through questioning, with care taken to provide for security in their own developing skills through a positive response to drawings that look simplistic from an adult point of view. In making, their products may not look very much like their designs. Young children may be encouraged to draw before making in order to develop the skills of visualisation. Younger children may include themselves in the picture (Ritchie 1995). For many young children, drawing must follow the act of making in order for them to be able to visualise what the materials can do (Anning 1993, Constable 1994b).

The purpose of completing such an activity will be to focus the child on the parts in their model, and possibly to provide a design for another child to follow. The approach is suitable for older children when using construction kits to explore mechanisms, for example. The drawings serve the purpose of identifying the various movements of components (Garvey 1995). Gradually children in Key Stage 1 will learn to annotate their drawings with the names of the different components, and later the techniques they will use in making the products. This places the purpose of the design into the context of the whole project. They are not just designing to produce a picture for the wall, but to use as their guide for making. Some young children will use their drawings almost instinctively, but others will require adult support and guidance to encourage purposeful use. A useful approach is to suggest that the child imagine that another person will make their model so the annotations have to be useful and clear. A similar approach applies to exploded diagrams when the focus may be very much on components and fixing techniques.

Floor plans and side elevations

Accurately measured floor plans or side elevations require a higher level of mathematical skill and very good visualisation of the product. Side elevations on a house plan usually include external features and internal cross-sections. Children from age three to eight usually have little difficulty with the notion of side elevations from an external aesthetic viewpoint. This is the type of drawing that many of them produce when asked to draw a house. However, there are sometimes difficulties with perspective when drawing the roof or a porch. More problems arise with helping children in the younger age range to visualise floor plans and cross-sections, but there are very simple methods to aid progression here. A toy house in a reception classroom, for example, will provide a cross-sectional view. It is useful to open the front and attach a large piece of paper, then use a wax crayon to rub an image of the edges of the walls and floor onto the paper. In this way, the children may view a cross-section as drawn. At this stage, one may not expect all the children to complete their own cross-sectional drawing.

Looking at floor plans using building bricks to create the walls of a building is a similar process. When children construct a house, they can be encouraged to look down on the construction as if they are birds in the sky as in Figure 2.5. To record what they see and to provide a plan view of their construction a wax rubbing is useful as in Figure 2.6. When the house is complete the children will form a better conceptual understanding of the relationship between the two-dimensional plan, and the three-dimensional construction.

Another way to approach this is to use the 'bedroom in a shoebox' idea demonstrated below. The child may design and make their ideal bedroom in a shoebox. If one opens the box by cutting the corners the child will be able to see the relationship between a three-dimensional view (Figure 2.7) and a two-dimensional view of the room (Figure 2.8). This may then lead into the drawing of simple plans and elevations at a later stage.

Figure 2.5 Constructing walls – aerial view

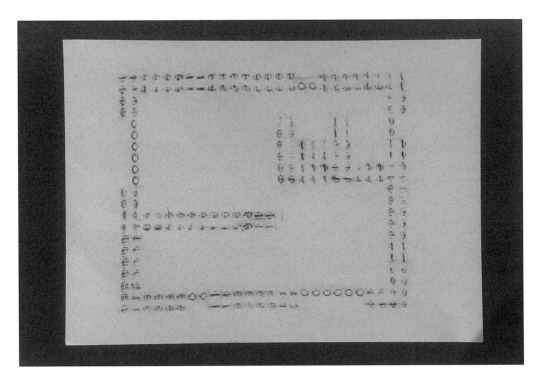

Figure 2.6 A plan made by wax rubbing

Children benefit from seeing actual house plans, and instructions for fixing self-assembly units together. First experiences of aerial views are often on playmats in nursery and reception, board games and train tracks. Sometimes these are confusing because the mats often have pictures on them in side elevation while roads are in aerial view. Block printing or sticky paper shapes will also create room plans. The spaces between the shapes represent the walls. Similarly, a simple graphics program is useful (see Figure 2.9).

Experiences of aerial views are essential to young children's understanding of plans

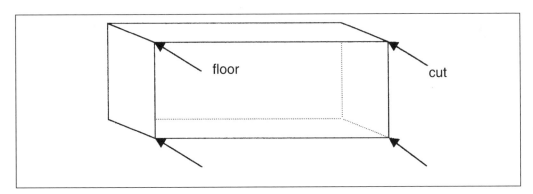

Figure 2.7 A room in a shoebox – oblique aerial view

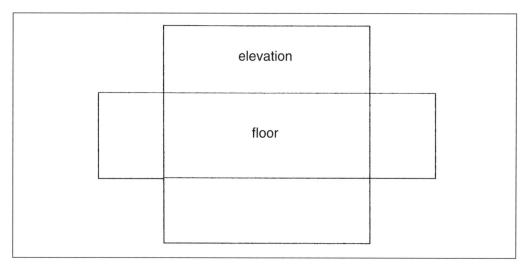

Figure 2.8 The shoebox opened

(Gardner 1995). Some older children may also be able to develop ideas about simple orthographic projections, building on previous experiences of drawing from different viewpoints. Teacher Activity 7 helps to develop ideas about orthographic projections in a relatively simple way.

Scale drawings

Understanding the concept of scale begins in sorting activities in the early years of school. Children recognise that shapes can be the same while the size changes. In design and technology, the experience of scale becomes more relevant by exploring stories such as The Three Bears (see Figure 2.10). The children may make chairs of the same shape and style but different sizes, from construction kits. They will then begin to recognise numerical relationships in the numbers of pieces used for a particular part of the chair.

When creating a 'home' for a toy, young children will become aware of the need to

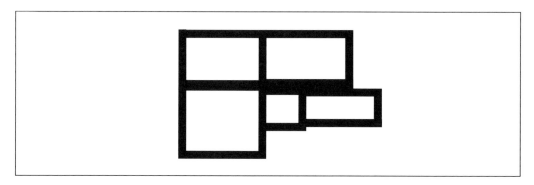

Figure 2.9 Shapes create room plans using a simple graphics program

Teacher Activity 7 – A new bedroom

Aim:
To understand the relationship between two-dimensional and three-dimensional modelling of side elevations.

Resources:
- orthographic projection sheet
- scissors
- drawing implements
- squared paper
- a selection of small cuboid boxes.

Task:

1. Cut the orthographic projection sheet along the solid lines and fold along the dotted lines. You may now view the proposed room elevations from either the inside or the outside.

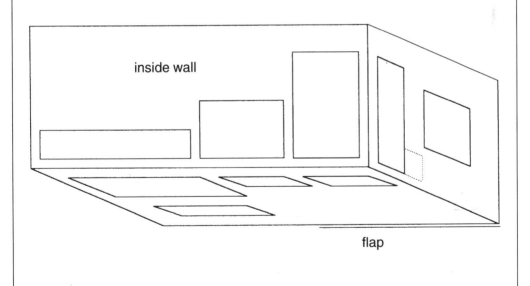

inside wall

flap

2. Choose a small box and a sheet of squared paper. Draw 'axes' across the centre of the squared paper to create four quadrants. Using the orthographic projection sheet as an example, create your own orthographic projection for the cuboid box. The squares are a useful guide. Include the main graphic detail such as lettering.

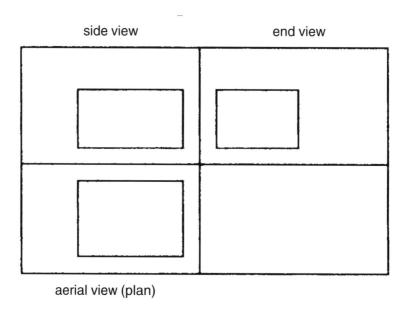

side view   end view

aerial view (plan)

3. Now cut and fold to explore the three-dimensional image. Compare it with the actual box. Is your drawing accurate?

Orthographic projection sheet

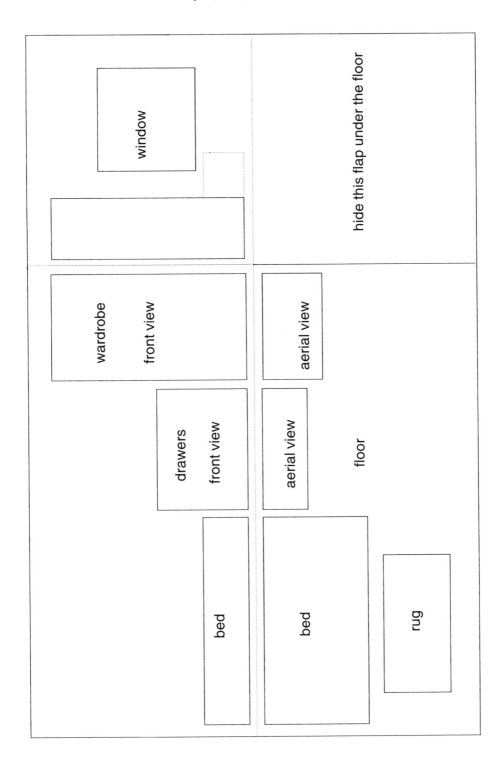

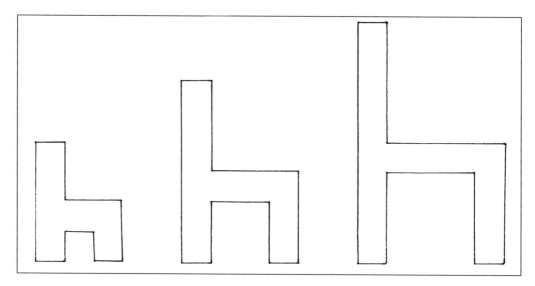

Figure 2.10 Side elevations of The Three Bears' chairs

create doors and windows that are of an appropriate size. Thus ideas of scale develop early on, although the children may still be using trial and error methods, and measuring by comparison in their approach to designing and making. Later in their schooling children will be introduced to geographical and mathematical procedures associated with scale and will recognise that most designs are drawn to a much smaller scale than real life. For many children making a model, the designs may be the actual size. Until children have sufficient accuracy of measurement in 'actual size' designs there is little point focusing on developing ideas in a different scale. However, the use of different sizes of squared paper to explore scaling is very appropriate before attempting to design to a smaller scale on plain paper. The same product made in several different scales, e.g. a range of gift boxes, plant pots or festive decorations, reinforces the need to be able to transfer to different scales. Wallpaper and coordinated furnishing designs often feature the same design in different sizes and provide a relevant and useful resource. Isometric paper of different scales is useful for developing similar ideas in three dimensions. When children understand scale and have appropriate accuracy in measuring skills they may complete a more demanding project. For example, they could design and make a puppet theatre for a specific size of puppet, using accurately scaled drawings. Perspective drawing is another specialist technique to introduce to older children.

Modelling with 'mock-ups'

The limited amount of time allocated to design and technology in primary schools often means that children are not provided with sufficient opportunity to practise skills and try out new ideas before making the final product. With the emphasis on modelling through drawing, children often fail to fulfil their design proposals, often because they are too complex, or because the modes of fixing and methods used have not been researched. Through modelling with 'mock-ups', children may make mistakes without fear of wasting good materials, or the disappointment of making a mess of a product after many hours of hard work. Initially, mocking up for young children might be placing a piece of card to see if it fits and produces the desired effect. It might include gesture, bending paper and trying to visualise what will happen. Visualising is clearly in three dimensions, which for primary age children is more appropriate than two dimensions.

Shaping with mouldable materials

For very young children, shaping a product with a mouldable material may be very useful in developing design ideas. For example, the children may make a simple vehicle chassis as a focused task, followed by the development of a body for the vehicle. Making the vehicle body from a mouldable material allows immediate adaptation of shape and size to suit the chassis. Children will make use of such a shape in a variety of ways. It provides a template to create a paper net by drawing around the base and the sides and by taking a strip of paper the width of the model across the top. The paper pieces will fix together and further shaping takes place as required. Mouldable materials also provide a mould for papier mâché models. The first layer of paper is attached to the mould by greasing it; then the papier mâché is applied. When the papier mâché dries, it slips easily off the mould to provide the basis of a very strong vehicle body to attach the chassis to. It is possible to cut windows out of the body but not easily and safely. Older children will plan for placing windows and prepare the mould accordingly. Moulding a raised portion in the shape of the window is one method. The next challenge is to create something for the interior. Younger children may create a 'solid' body then add aesthetic features, such as windows, to the surface using any suitable media. When varnished, such a vehicle is usually strong, safe and aesthetically pleasing. With a mould of this type there is the potential to produce several vehicle bodies of the same size and shape, thus introducing the children to mass production techniques. This type of project has potential when setting up a toyshop for role-play activities, for school funds.

Trying out ideas with construction kits

For all ages construction kits lend themselves to a variety of approaches in primary design and technology. There is usually an element of free play necessary, but for design and technology, the use is specific to the task. Making an item with the kit is not an end in itself, but is for purposeful enquiry of a particular structure or mechanism. Once children have undertaken such enquiry then it is feasible that such structures and mechanisms can be included in their own designs. The kit allows rapid exploration of features, and again avoids mistakes when using the final material. For example, prior to constructing a wooden chassis for a vehicle children may explore a chassis made from a kit in order to determine which features they wish to incorporate, and which are undesirable in a different material. In a similar way to the approach suggested with mouldable materials, a kit may help to formulate ideas about the shape of the vehicle body. Figure 2.11 shows the use of a set of interlocking bricks to create such a body. This provides a template to create a net from squared paper (see Figure 2.12), and then the final net with tabs added from card. The net scales up or down with ease, using different sizes of squared paper.

Figure 2.11 A vehicle body from interlocking bricks

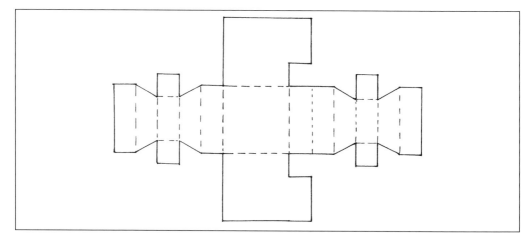

Figure 2.12 A net drawn from the model in Figure 2.11

Temporary fixings

Masking tape is a cheap and invaluable resource that is fast becoming part of every teacher's basic kit. Learning how to use temporary joins allows time for evaluation of the product while in the designing stage. There is nothing worse than discovering that a specific part of a product has been glued too soon, restricting the addition of another. The use of paper and masking tape to mock up prospective card products, such as gift boxes, allows constant readjustment in measurements before a commitment to the final design. At the later stage before finally gluing the card, paper clips are useful to hold the box in shape while checking its construction. Minor alterations are then possible without damaging the surface of the final product. Similarly, when designing pop-up cards, interior additions require temporary fixing with a substance such as Blu-tak to ensure they fit within the card when closed.

Modelling a system as part of a design

A window is a readily available resource to demonstrate the principles of a simple system. A simple system has the following components:

INPUT ⟶ PROCESS ⟶ OUTPUT

Very simply, the person opening the window supplies the input. The process is the opening action of the handle or stay and the window perhaps describing an arc. The output is the open window, with the stay holding it in place to let air in the room. To close the window the system reverses. An opportunity to explore simple systems arises when children engage in creating a 'home' for a toy or a vehicle that has opening windows.

It is advisable to try out different ideas for the mechanisms by which the windows will open before finalising product designs. Working models provide the opportunity to ensure that the idea will work, and help to develop new ideas and improvements through evaluation. For example, suitable components for the windows and their mechanisms are the first consideration. Secondly comes consideration of the input, and this may be a pushing, a pulling or a sliding action. Several levels of difficulty in producing such a window system are observable. Focusing on the window as a system avoids over-emphasis on the aesthetic features of the product. Teacher Activity 8 provides an opportunity to reflect on an activity at several different levels of complexity. The importance of looking at specific aspects in this way is that it enables reflection upon classroom practice. For example, if there are children capable of the simplest method without any assistance then opportunity for teaching a new skill arises. Individual children extend their skills, rather than repeating skills of which they are already capable.

Simple nets

The visualisation of the relationship between three-dimensional shapes and two-dimensional nets is problematic. The links with mathematics are clear and children in

Teacher Activity 8 – Modelling window systems

Aim: To develop an understanding of how to complete the same task with different levels of complexity.

Task:

Read the following suggested progression for developing skills in modelling window systems as a focused task for a design-and-make task that requires the children to build a house from card. It may be useful to model these ideas in card yourself.

(a) Discuss whether you agree or disagree with the proposed progression and provide reasons for your decisions.

(b) Add further steps to the progression at any point on the continuum.

(c) Discuss how you may implement focused tasks that enable children to make progress in their capability.

Suggested progression for modelling window systems:

- Draw a window on the card wall of the house and cut along three edges with scissors to allow a fold along the fourth edge to create a hinge.

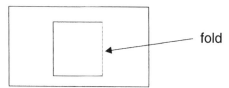

fold

- Using a paper drill and scissors cut a hole in the card where the window will be. Create a frame from card for the window. Stick Perspex to the frame and attach the frame to the house using sticky tape. Use Velcro as a fastener.

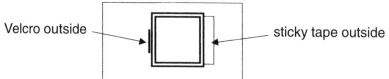

Velcro outside   sticky tape outside

- Follow the same procedure as above but make two frames that allow the Perspex to be sandwiched between them. Create a hinge from a plastic straw and florists' wire. Make a handle from a split pin.

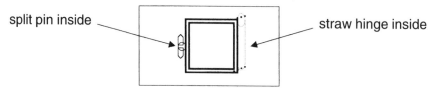

split pin inside   straw hinge inside

Reflection:

- How will you know when to stimulate further challenges?
- What questions might you ask? What suggestions will you make?

Key Stage 1 will have some experience of some links. For example, they may know that the face of a cuboid is a rectangle. Nets are commonly introduced at around the age of seven and children may explore how boxes open out into flat composite shapes that fix together with flaps. Later, children are usually more able to create their own nets to make specific geometrical shapes. Much of this work may take place within the context of a design-and-make project in which children make a gift box, e.g. an Easter egg box, for a specific product. In design and technology, the term for a net is a 'development', possibly derived from the idea that in designing it one is 'developing' a net. Simple nets such as cubes and cuboids cause few problems at ages seven to eleven, but the composite shapes require thoughtful developments to aid progression.

One interesting and relatively simple way to explore the development of nets is to use a graphics package that allows rapid drawing of simple shapes. Figure 2.13 is created from five rectangles.

Before using a graphics package, very young children benefit from the use of sticky paper shapes to create their net. Providing the appropriate materials and design tools aids progressive development in understanding the dimensional relationships. Child Activity 9 helps the teacher explore how children respond to using a simple graphics program to create a net. Presentation of the activity to the children will depend upon their age and experience. The work card on the sheet suits older children.

Some publications provide a range of templates for activities, similar to the one provided for the simple platform pop-up card. Providing templates of nets will not necessarily help children to develop their own skills but when used to help them understand complex nets they are a valid teaching aid. This type of template use is really an extension of a child opening a food packet to explore its construction. It provides a model that children may modify and develop. Eventually children will be able to design their own from the beginning. Figures 2.14 and 2.15 provide a simple example of how a child may use the previous knowledge of a given net template to progress individual skill in developing.

Using designs to inform making

Too often designing in primary schools becomes an activity that fails to inform the product. The design is drawn and put away; then the real activity of making begins. By now readers are aware that the two processes are not distinct and that one cannot

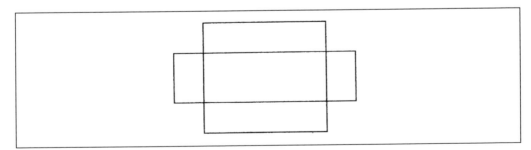

Figure 2.13 A simple net for an open box

Child Activity 9 – Using Information Technology to create a net

Aim: For the teacher to observe children working with two-dimensional images that will create a three-dimensional form.

Resources:

- any graphics package with which the children are familiar; it must be capable of drawing regular shapes
- scrap paper
- card
- scissors
- masking tape
- glue.

Task: Within a context appropriate to the age and interests of the children, set a design-and-make task that will result in the children creating a net for a small box, e.g.:

The school is having a spring fete at which the children will sell small boxes containing individual portions of homemade biscuits. The target customers are the children who might buy a box as a small gift for an adult. The children are to design and make gift boxes to hold three biscuits.

Designing a box

What do you need to know?

- the client
- the size of the contents
- the materials available.

Of what do you need to think?

- people's needs
- size
- colour
- shape
- materials
- cost.

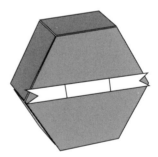

Challenges:

- Try to put a window in the lid.
- Try to design a box that is good value for money.

Reflection:

- How do the children respond to the task?
- What difficulties arise and how do you help the children to overcome them?
- Did children make significant progress in any particular aspect?

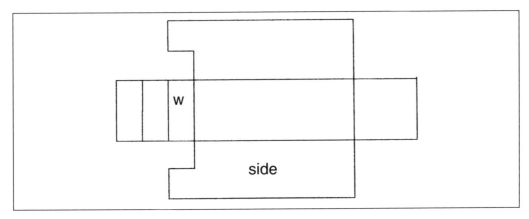

Figure 2.14 A net for a lorry with vertical windscreen (no tabs added) (w)

operate without the other. For younger children the act of making might be more important but designing is still happening in a very imaginative and intuitive way. It is all in the mind, and epitomises the notion of interaction between hand and eye. Teacher Activity 10 is designed to focus attention on a variety of approaches to modelling vehicle bodies, before considering in more detail how the process of modelling relates to that of making.

An important point is that no clear-cut age-related progression exists, although there may be general trends. Another important feature is that there are many ways in which modelling can occur. For children to make progress they need experience of many different approaches to modelling. The experiences they gain will depend on the materials available and the design-and-make tasks undertaken. The design process will encompass many aspects of modelling.

The purpose of designing is to create a product that has a particular purpose and is suited to the needs of the user. For young children this may be a user within the realms of fantasy or a toy. Younger children will find designing and making for themselves much easier than for others. Progress in developing designs and using them to inform

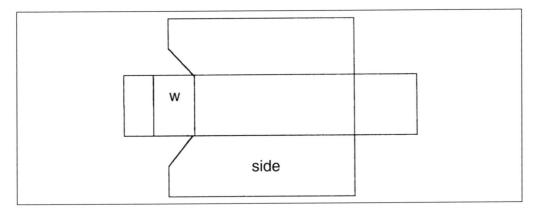

Figure 2.15 Modified net providing 45° angled windscreen (w)

Teacher Activity 10 – Thinking 'progression'

Aim: To consider detailed elements of progression inherent in the task of modelling a vehicle body before making.

Resources:

- photocopies of the statements below
- scissors
- plain paper.

Task:

(a) Cut the sheet into strips and place the strips in an order that you think represents a suitable progression.
(b) Use some empty strips of paper to add further detail to the progression.

Some ideas for modelling vehicle bodies:

Build a solid shape from Multilink and use it as a template for the cardboard sides, front, back and roof
Stick cardboard boxes together with masking tape
Model door hinges and choose the most suitable for the vehicle
Discuss as a group how a box might be modified by adding parts using temporary fixings
Use accurate drawing techniques to create a net for the vehicle
Bend, fold and rotate thick paper to aid visualisation of the shape
Draw separate front, side and rear views of the car. Fix them together with masking tape to determine the size of the roof
Show an adult helper where to cut a window after modelling it with paper and Blu-tak
Make a shell from a suitable construction kit
Create a template from a side view of the vehicle drawn on a simple graphics package

making relies heavily on the children becoming capable of setting design criteria. Once children begin to set their own design criteria they become much more aware of the purpose of the designing process in relation to making. Children set their own design criteria from an early age, but not in any formal sense. Four-year-old children are capable of making decisions about their products. Designing at this stage is very closely interwoven with making as children will design 'in their heads' as they choose the materials and tools for the product.

One might provide five-year-old children with the necessary materials and tools to make puppets. They will discuss their ideas for products with an adult and design through discussion, choosing, modelling by gesture, and by 'mocking up' with the actual materials. Slightly older children at six will be capable of drawing their puppet before making and will use their design to help them make the product. At this age, the thought given to the exact materials for the final product is limited. For example, a child might draw a puppet with spiky hair, but then have difficulty in creating the same type of spiky hair in practice. Children are very inventive, and will use whatever is available, modify it to suit their needs and be satisfied with the result. To provide encouragement to follow designs more closely, the teacher might set up projects with a clear focus on providing examples of specific features. Children designing a house might be given pictures of different shapes of roofs, and make 'mock-ups' in paper to explore the three-dimensional forms. By the age of eight one might expect children to annotate design drawings with confidence, to consider how they are going to fix parts together and to use the drawing to inform making.

As we have found earlier, though, the relationship between 'designing' and 'making' is a complex one and making often precedes designing (Johnsey 1997) especially in the introduction of new materials. Hence, opportunities for exploration of new materials and tools must be available for children of all ages before designing. Alongside this is the need for focused tasks that provide the necessary experiences in a structured way to allow application and progressive development by the children. Children making packaging for an Easter egg benefit from exploring the mathematical aspects of packaging first (Chalkley and Shield 1996). This provides the necessary background knowledge and understanding. To develop their designing skills further they also need experiences with mathematical construction materials, e.g. 'Clixi' or 'Polydron', that allow quick and easy development of nets.

Finally, Teacher Activity 11 is to focus attention on modelling with mock-ups, making use of information gathered from other sources. The result of this activity provides the template for making a product in Teacher Activity 17. This is a clear opportunity to use the design to inform making. Children have this opportunity too in using their graphic design of a net for a gift box, during Child Activity 16.

Teacher Activity 11 – A 'dream car'

Aim: To develop skills in modelling with mock-ups.

Resources:
- drawing paper
- sugar paper
- squared paper
- scissors
- masking tape
- a vehicle chassis made from a construction kit.

Scene:

You are a designer who is competing against others to produce a marketable design for a 'dream car'. This is not an easy task because everyone will have different preferences. Your aim is to produce an idea that appeals to those people who are in the higher income bracket and can afford to be a little extravagant.

Task:

1. Consider the shape of vehicle bodies by looking at pictures, or by observing cars parked outside. Note detailed features and consider reasons for their shape, size and orientation, e.g. windows, door handles.
2. Sketch your dream car. Consider carefully the shape of the body and its features.
3. Make a paper mock-up of the body that will fit the provided chassis.

- You may use any process you choose to aid visualisation of the vehicle.
- Use sugar paper or squared paper for the mock-up.
- Masking tape is the temporary fixing.

The result should open out into a single development to enable the creation of the final product in Teacher Activity 17.

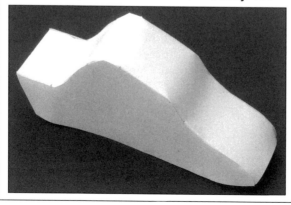

Figure 2.16 A simple paper mock-up

Chapter 3

Making

Using 'found' materials

Funding levels in many schools unfortunately result in a lack of specialist resources for design and technology. Children often complete design and make projects with 'found' materials and schools must consider how progressive development of the use of such materials may occur. This is not a suggestion that such materials are the only ones in use, nor that they are desirable. When they are used, teachers are to consider the development of quality products while at the same time making efforts to improve the resource levels.

Activity 12 focuses attention on a cereal box to create a product. The choice of topic will fit with the curriculum of the school. The box may become part of a building, a vehicle, a lunch box, a medical kit or a piece of furniture, for example. Of utmost importance when considering progression, is the manner in which the box is used, and ways of modifying it to meet the purpose of the product. Attention to the quality of product is essential, in terms of both function and aesthetics. Function is the domain of design and technology while focusing on aesthetic finishing techniques creates a clear link with the art and design curriculum. Later in the chapter there is further discussion of the idea of 'quality' in relation to processes, products and progression.

Considering the process of making provides the opportunity to explore in more depth the relationships between skills, knowledge and understanding. Chapter 1 included an overview of the relationships and suggested that development of conceptual understanding in design and technology is through the application of both skill and knowledge to the task. Activity 12 requires a focus on the three main strands of progression and consideration of the teacher's role in enabling progress.

Clarifying ideas about how children use materials is an important part of planning by the teacher. Children can move towards better quality process and products through the teacher's own skills, knowledge and understanding of the task. This is not a suggestion that children will all make the same product and have the same outcome, merely that teachers ought to be aware of the possible outcomes that exist. A guided approach enables progression on an individual level while a didactic approach relies on progression by task clearly controlled by the teacher. One danger in using found

Teacher/Child Activity 12 – The ubiquitous cereal box

Aim: To consider progressive development in using 'found' materials to produce quality products at any level.

Resources:

- cereal boxes
- scissors
- masking tape
- newsprint or 'kitchen' paper
- PVA glue and spreaders
- paints, felt-tip pens and other graphic media.

Task:

(a) How might you expect a child to make use of the cereal box in:

Reception

Year 3

Year 6?

(b) Take a box into the classroom and ask the children how they might use it in a particular product.
- What differences exist in the children's ideas at different ages?

- What evidence exists of previous experiences influencing suggestions?

- What is the role of the teacher in helping children to develop ideas to extend their conceptual development, in making use of previous skills, knowledge and understanding?

materials much of the time is that the child does not make good progress but remains almost at the same level throughout their schooling. While their models may become more complex, their use of materials may not make progress if they rely completely on the shape of the 'found' materials to dictate the shape of the outcome. For example, a child of five will make a box into a car, almost oblivious to the shape of a real car. Their imagination allows them to perceive the box as a car. A child at ten may still make a box into a car but the addition of axles and wheels might be more sophisticated. The addition of another box to create a more realistic shape might also be a possibility. There might be opening windows and doors. The aesthetic features may be better quality, but the original shapes of the boxes remain and therefore the model still lacks realism.

A child who has made progress by age ten will cut, shape and remodel the box until it becomes the required shape for a more realistic model of a car based on observational drawings. There will be a clear attempt to ensure the final product has no remnants of the original material 'giving the game away'. The overall functional and aesthetic quality will be excellent.

The product to be made also influences how the 'found' material is used. A seven-

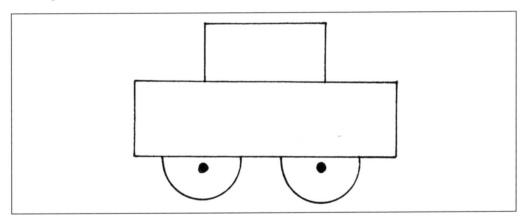

Figure 3.1 Making use of existing qualities

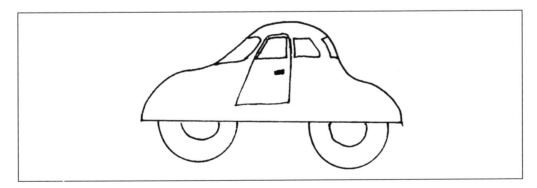

Figure 3.2 Reshaping the box for better realism

year-old child, who designed and made a mask from a cereal packet, clearly saw the packet as a source of flat card, nothing more. However, the same activity with a ten-year-old resulted in a three-dimensional mask that made use of the three-dimensional qualities provided by the box. In consideration of which child demonstrates the greater conceptual understanding, one must refer to the child's previous development. The relationships are complex and judgements are impossible on one project alone. The seven-year-old clearly viewed the box as a source of material and took little notice of its original form. The ten-year-old made good use of the three-dimensional qualities, but retained the shape instead of modifying it.

Progression in making

Previous paragraphs suggest some ideas for considering progression with 'found' materials, and encourage a focus on the development of conceptual understanding through application of skills and knowledge to a design-and-make task. In Chapter 2 the focus is not as explicit. However, in providing 'challenges', as in designing the pop-up card in Teacher/Child Activity 3, in meeting the challenge the child is applying knowledge and skill learned from the previous simpler mechanism. Teacher Activity 13 explores the theme of vehicle building for which specific examples are included in Chapter 2. Participants will generate suggestions for different ways of building vehicles in Activity 13. The suggestions when analysed will provide a broad developmental progression for vehicle building.

Completing the chart will develop expertise in identifying different strands of progression. That skills and knowledge contribute to developing conceptual understanding is clear (see Figure 3.3).

Vehicles are a popular design-and-make task, often as part of a scientific exploration of forces and energy, or the design and technology strand of the theme 'Transport'. The identification of a broad progression is easy. One may expect, for example, that very young children will make a vehicle with fixed wheels, while an older child will create one with moving wheels. One might fine-tune and expect the development of a moving axle and wheels to be superseded by the fixed axle and moving wheels. Progression can never be a static order of development, because so much depends on the actual materials used and the context. The classroom context affects the nature of the progression as well as the topical context in which the project is set. While it is possible to identify strands within a specific project, whether a child progresses towards these, or indeed beyond them, depends upon the quality of teacher intervention during the activity.

Teacher intervention focuses the child's attention and develops thinking about the process (Bennett 1996). For example, in using a large box for a vehicle in imaginary play, children may demonstrate that they know the position of the steering wheel. They may open and close windows and toot the horn. They may not realise that a car has an accelerator pedal or brakes. Adult intervention in the play situation may help the child focus on how the imaginary car starts and stops. Suitable questions might be: 'What makes the car go?' and 'How will the car stop?' Simple

Teacher Activity 13 – Progression in vehicle building

Aim: To develop further ideas about enabling progress in particular design and technology skills, knowledge and understanding during an activity to build a vehicle.

Resources:

- strips of paper and Blu-tak
- felt-tip pens.

Task:

- Each member of the group is to contribute a suggestion for developing ideas about vehicle building and to write it on a strip of paper, e.g.:

> Explore a rack and pinion steering mechanism using a construction kit, and then incorporate this into a model that steers around corners

> A large box becomes a vehicle in imaginary play

> Make a wooden 'Jinks' chassis as a focused task, and use a given cardboard net as the vehicle body

- Discuss the merits of each idea and attempt to put them into a progression.
- Create a chart of the skills, knowledge and understanding inherent in each idea.
- Identify any possible gaps in the progression and consider how you may implement these ideas in the classroom to cater for a range of needs.

Activity	Strands of progression		
	Skill	Knowledge	Understanding
A large box becomes a vehicle in imaginary play	Visualising the use of shape and space	That a vehicle often has a box-like shape	Demonstrating how a vehicle works, through imaginary play

	Strands of progression		
Activity	Skill	Knowledge	Understanding
Explore a rack and pinion steering mechanism using a construction kit, and then incorporate this into a model that steers round corners	Make a rack and pinion mechanism with the kit	Know how the mechanism works	Incorporate the mechanism into a working model

Figure 3.3 Identifying the strands of progression

questions such as these will generate a range of ideas for discussion with a group of children and in this way help them to make progress in understanding how a vehicle works. The opportunity to make and add working features to the boxcar will then lead to conceptual development. Next time the children design and make a vehicle the teacher may expect the application of the new skills and knowledge thus acquired.

Using tools

Teaching safe use of tools begins with under-fives. From the beginning children will learn how to be aware of their own safety and the safety of others. Some teachers are wary of using particular tools such as saws, hammers and various cutters. The reality is that for many children a sharp pencil may be a dangerous tool when not used properly. Children are not likely to hurt themselves with a saw when used correctly. Children vary enormously in their ability to use tools well at an early age. Much depends on the opportunities to experience the use of tools. A child who regularly uses scissors at home will be quite competent on arrival at school, while another child may not be. There is a general progression linked to the age and maturity of the child ranging from insensitive use of all tools through to sensitive handling of complex tools (drill, saw and jig, cutting knife, glue gun) (Lever 1990).

Unfortunately, some tools, such as saws, are used so infrequently that progress is unlikely. Neglect of teaching the correct use of other tools, such as the familiar pair of scissors, means children will fail to make much progress here too. The familiarity of scissors as a basic tool leads to inadequate teaching of skills. Too often adults assume that children acquire the skills without direct teaching. Correct use of a range of scissors is fundamental to many design-and-make activities in school. The following progression for their use might provide a model for identifying smaller steps in the use of other tools:

1. cutting play dough with blunt plastic scissors;
2. cutting into the edge of thin card with round-ended scissors;
3. cutting thin card into strips;
4. cutting along a straight line drawn on thin card;
5. cutting along a wavy line on thin card;
6. cutting round a circular object drawn on thin card;
7. cutting a zigzag pattern on thin card;
8. cutting a very detailed irregular design;
9. repeating steps 2 to 8 with thick paper;
10. repeating steps 2 to 8 with thin paper;
11. using wavy edge scissors accurately;
12. using utility snips to cut corrugated plastic sheets;
13. using textile shears with fabric;
14. using pinking shears with fabric;
15. cutting tissue paper.

Many children are competent in the first four listed skills when they enter school. At the other end of the continuum, opportunities to develop specialist skills with scissors may not exist in school. The list is not exhaustive and does not represent a linear progression that children must follow, but demonstrates that in learning the use of tools there are progressive factors to consider. The main factors are:

• increasing control;
• the nature of the materials to be cut;
• very small steps to allow consolidation;
• a wide range of experiences.

Specific skills must be taught, e.g. how best to cut round a circle with scissors. The progressive steps are not exhaustive. For example, the cutting of yarns, which young children have difficulty with, is not included. The size of the material is not mentioned. Young children have greater difficulty working with larger pieces of card or paper than with smaller ones for cutting. Just by looking at such a simple tool, one can see the complexity that arises in relation to progression. The result is a clear indication that broad Key Stages cannot identify detailed progression, nor can the progression be the same for each child. Progression in developing skills in the use of tools relates clearly to individual experience and teacher intervention. Research has shown that non-intervention creates a situation of failure, as children struggle to realise their designs without the necessary skills (Thompson 1990). Thompson was particularly concerned that if the focus were on skill development and adult conceptions of the product then children's originality would be stifled. However, children need teacher intervention for teaching specific skills. Teacher intervention thus aids the development of originality.

The focus so far is on skill development with tools. Knowledge and conceptual development are equally important. Knowledge about tools and their use leads to safe practice. Choosing which tool to use for a particular purpose is the application of knowledge and skill and therefore constitutes conceptual development. In teaching children the skill of using a tool, knowledge about the tool and its safe use will be essential. The skill and knowledge may be taught through focused tasks, e.g. each child learning how to cut a piece of 1 cm square section wood using a saw and bench hook. Application of that skill and knowledge in a design-and-make task follows. Alternatively, there is teaching of the necessary skill and knowledge required for the task. The former method ensures that all children have an opportunity to learn about the tool, while the latter provides for relevant and appropriate use for individual children. Both approaches are useful in the classroom, with successful outcomes in relation to progression for individual children.

The danger of the latter approach is that some children fail to gain experience with particular tools as they choose to design and make without them. Alternatively, the teacher fails to intervene at the point where a particular tool will be useful. To alleviate pressure on the teacher or other adult in the room, children may be encouraged to peer-teach, as long as the 'teacher' does not take over the task.

The risk of accidents when using dangerous tools such as knives is minimised, by following necessary safety procedures. The emphasis here is on correct and safe use of tools. For example, when working with food, children of all ages must learn the safest way to use knives. Knives need to be sharp enough to cut well and a serrated 'vegetable' knife is often the safest and most appropriate for many uses. Often, young children have table knives to cut vegetables such as potatoes. This practice is more dangerous than providing a sharper more suitable knife. Many table knives, particularly those in school, are for cutting soft cooked food and using them for hard items sometimes results in the knife slipping onto the child's fingers. To increase the safety of using knives there are various tools on the market that will hold food while it is cut, thus keeping fingers out of the way. Always teach children to cut down towards the chopping board and not towards the body or fingers.

The previous paragraphs provide a model for looking at progressive skill development that applies to a range of tools. Teacher Activity 14 provides the opportunity to reflect on how to intervene in the classroom situation where tool use is ineffective or incorrect. The 'situation' cards provide a focus for discussion.

Issues arising from the activity suggest teachers knowing the small steps of progression to improve a child's skill level. Teachers should know correct procedures for the use of tools, and consider provision for children who prefer to use their left hand. Practising the use of each tool with the less favoured hand is a very useful approach and the tool is easy to demonstrate either way. Most tools are designed for right-handed people, and the expectation is that left-handed people just have to learn how to work in that way. A drill handle, for example, turns in a clockwise direction and this means that the left hand turns it towards the body rather than away from the body. This is not the natural tendency. One can only understand the implications by trying it out. Some tools however may be bought especially for left-handed use, e.g. scissors, and others may be altered to suit either hand, e.g. most circular cutters. Others may suit either hand anyway, e.g. perforation cutters. When teaching the safe use of tools and their applications all these points must be borne in mind. Children also have difficulties

Teacher Activity 14 – Cutting interventions

Aim: To aid progress in specific skills for individual children within the classroom situation.

Resources:

• 'Situation' cards.

Task:

Take each card and consider the best response to the child's use of tools. Justify your response in terms of developing skills, knowledge or understanding.

'Situation' cards

Photocopy onto card

1 You see a right-handed child cutting round a circle in a clockwise direction	2 A child is stabbing a hole in a piece of card with scissors
3 A junior hacksaw used in the horizontal position to cut a piece of dowel held vertically in a vice	4 Craft knives in use with a plastic ruler to cut thin card
5 A left-handed child is using a circular cutter set for a right-handed grip	6 Wavy scissors are used but fail to produce a continuous pattern
7 The paper tears as the child is cutting	8 Pastry cutters are twisted when making biscuits
9 Fabric has frayed on the hem of a puppet	10 Use of the paper trimmer has left the sheets of thin card too small for the task
11 Finished pop-up birthday cards are of poor quality because the folds in the card are not 'sharp'	12 A circular hole in thick card, cut with scissors, is not accurate enough for the purpose of the product

when they fail to choose the correct tool for the job, demonstrating a lack of knowledge or understanding. Yet another problem is that of poor quality tools, e.g. blunt scissors. Poor quality tools will produce poor quality results even when a child has excellent skill levels.

Textiles

Textiles are a neglected medium in the primary curriculum. Often their use is limited to the creation of two-dimensional collage that is strictly speaking not design and technology. However, some educationists believe that such activity helps to progress children's ideas of choosing the most suitable fabric for the task (Stein and Poole 1997). In the past, primary school girls often created items using various textiles and yarns through knitting and sewing activities. The boys completed basketwork and woodwork. During that era, the purpose of teaching such crafts to primary school children was clearly to prepare them for perceived adult gender roles. Thankfully, such practice in school is outdated, and there is now equal opportunity to develop a range of skills.

Sewing and knitting have become hobby crafts for many people rather than essential skills and so engaging in creative design-and-make tasks with various textiles is often an exciting experience for the children in school. There is a therapeutic element to such tasks too, and children who are disruptive during other activities seem to show improved behaviour through engaging with textiles. The level of concentration required to develop textile skills transfers to other subject areas, and the level of satisfaction with a quality end-product seems all the greater because of the effort involved in making. Designing and making with textiles encompasses a broad knowledge and understanding of the nature and purpose of textiles for different purposes.

Two specific aspects may be developed within a design-and-make task:

- constructing textiles – e.g. weaving, knitting, knotting, braiding;
- constructing with textiles – e.g. sewing, gluing.

Both activities will mostly culminate in the creation of three-dimensional structures. For example, a shoulder strap woven for a bag becomes part of the whole structure. Weaving a piece of fabric that is not destined for use as a product is a craft activity. When incorporated into a product it becomes design and technology. The focus in a textile activity is on joining threads, fibres and fabrics in any combination (Bottrill 1994).

Weaving activities will exemplify some aspects of progression. Weaving is a challenging construction activity. Children often produce weaving that results in uneven tension (Hardcastle 1994). To alleviate the problem, Hardcastle suggests teaching the warp and weft skills separately. For example, children may draw threads from some loose hessian observing what happens. They will then weave into the hessian some threads of their own. Pieces created in such a way may become part of a product, such as a shoe bag or a cushion. Weaving into a variety of nets is the next step.

This could include stiffer netting such as chicken wire for more rigid structures. To practise skill involving the warp threads, children may create 'wrappings' of threads around card, based on their observations of colour and texture in a picture. It is easier for children to work on a peg or 'speed' loom to complete their first weaving (see Figure 3.4). The warp threads attach to the pegs and they hang down to any length required. The child weaves in and out of the pegs. When several rows are complete the pegs lift up and the weft slides down onto the warp. Such a loom helps to avoid over tightening of the weft and produces a more even piece. Many teachers will not have access to such a loom and may prefer to work with card looms in the first instance.

Card looms are simple for children to make and use (see Figure 3.5). With a little help children as young as five may make and use such a loom. For the youngest children corrugated card is useful because it is strong, but may be difficult to cut. The warp threads will be approximately two centimetres apart and will be in two colours.

The two warp colours help the child recognise whether to weave over or under the

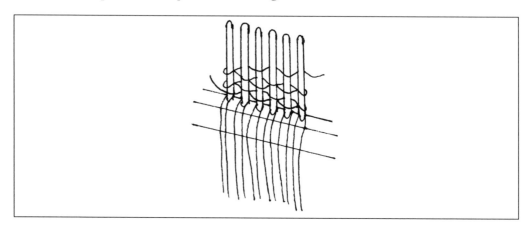

Figure 3.4 A peg loom

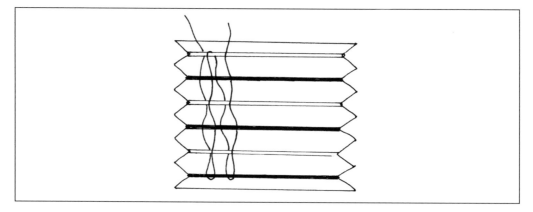

Figure 3.5 A simple card loom

thread. This will produce a very loosely woven fabric. As the child matures then the width between the threads may lessen and the necessity for the two colours will disappear. Whatever the approach the nature of the progression should always depend upon the capability of the child. Children are to be encouraged to design before making, through reference to pictures and colour swatches that identify their choices. It is easier to design using the weft threads initially, and then later children may consider the effects of changing the colour of the warp threads. The warp threads become more evident when very close together as on a simple lollipop stick loom (see Figure 3.6).

In sewing fabrics during a design-and-make task, the following lines of progression require consideration:

- size and type of needle, e.g. large and blunt to small and pointed;
- size and type of yarn, e.g. thicker and stronger to thinner and weaker;
- type of fabric, e.g. large open weave to close weave.

Sewing skills may follow a progressive development:

1. threading beads on a lace;
2. sewing cards with laces;
3. sewing cards using wool and large plastic needles;
4. sewing running stitch in Binca with a bodkin and wool;
5. developing a range of stitches on Binca;

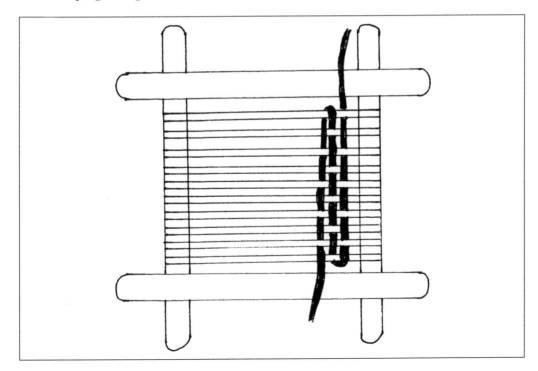

Figure 3.6 Close weaving on a simple loom

6. sewing on hessian with an embroidery needle and thread
7. using fine needle and thread to gather fabric with running stitch.

There are bound to be other steps between and certainly more steps to add. There is difficulty in fitting such skills as threading one's own needle and learning starting and finishing techniques into the progression. These experiences will be slightly different with different needles, yarns and fabrics. For such skills, the essential point to remember is that children ought to be taught them at all stages, using appropriate methods. Very young children may fasten their wool to the Binca with masking tape. When the line of sewing is finished the children will learn how to sew in the ends. Later the children will learn how to sew two firm stitches into the fabric, thus holding it in place. Large needles are usually easy to thread, but for those who have difficulties, a simple needle-threading tool is appropriate.

One might also consider the colouring or enhancing of fabrics before making is also a valid activity as part of a design-and-make task (Bell 1996). Colouring and enhancing fabric to create a particular effect, for example when creating a costume for a play, are again part of art and design, but a clear link to the subject of design and technology. The difficulty is in defining a clear progression. One cannot, and much depends upon individual experiences. Fabric crayons and pens, for example, are useful for simple or complex designs by any age of child. However, one may not wish to explore the use of hot wax in Batik until children are in the upper years of the primary school and beyond because of the safety issues.

The main concern raised from observation of several textile activities in schools is that children rarely design the textile product before they make it. Child Activity 15 focuses on a very simple product to allow a focus on the process. Designing with fabrics suffers because the children do not have the knowledge and skills essential for the task. To provide the necessary experiences one must look closely at the task and the problems within it, then provide a means of overcoming the problems so the focus may be on the design. When children design on plain paper for some sewing to create a design on Binca, they have difficulty translating their picture into stitches. A photocopy or scanned picture of Binca provides an extremely useful and realistic design sheet on which children create the design stitch by stitch. Child Activity 15 provides such an example. From the photo (Figure 3.7), one may see the design clearly leads into making the product. It is another opportunity for children's ideas to progress in a structured way.

Sheet materials

In Chapter 2 a progression for the modelling of vehicle bodies was analysed and developed in Teacher Activity 10. The purpose of identifying such a progression is to provide the teacher with knowledge of the opportunities that exist, to challenge individual children to fulfil their potential. Either flexible sheet materials, e.g. thin card, or rigid sheet materials, e.g. corrugated plastic, are useful to construct the body of such a vehicle. The next two sections look at these two very different types of materials.

Child Activity 15 – Sewing by design

Aim: To observe young children creating their own designs for a simple product made from fabric.

Resources:

- Binca
- photocopied sheets of Binca
- felt-tip pens
- embroidery cottons and needles
- masking tape
- card
- glue.

Task:

(Try this activity throughout the school, but modify the approach to suit the children.)

1. Teach the children one or more simple stitches as a focused task, e.g. running stitch, backstitch and cross-stitch.
2. Decide on a simple product to design and make, e.g. a bookmark. Provide the children with a photocopy of the Binca on which they may design their product using coloured pens to match the threads.
3. Create the bookmark using the design as a guide. If glued onto card it provides a durable product with a high quality finish.

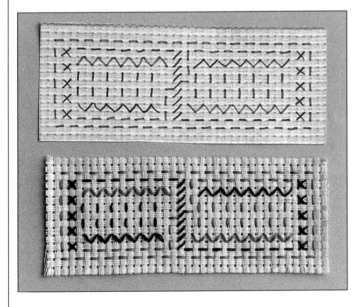

Figure 3.7 'Designing for making'

Discussion points:

- Were the children able to design on the photocopies?
- Did the children use their designs to inform their making?
- What modifications were necessary for five-year-old children? Ten-year-olds? (age group progression)
- What evidence was there of varying capability in the use of sewing skills in a class?
- What was the cause of variations? Any noticeable gender differences?
- How did you cater for the difference in skill level? (individual progression)

Flexible sheet materials

Children often use flexible sheet materials in a variety of activities that focus more on the aesthetic outcome. For design-and-make tasks, the focus will be on creating structures or mechanisms that become part of a product. In Teacher/Child Activity 3, the mechanism in the pop-up card is the folded platform. Children may be challenged to make the mechanism more complex as well as improving the aesthetic appeal of the card. Later will be the introduction of a selection of more challenging alternative styles of mechanisms to develop. Gradually children gain knowledge and understanding of a range of mechanisms allowing them to make choices. A net made from flexible sheet material will fold to create a structure. The strength of the material alters when its shape alters thus allowing it to become a shell structure for a vehicle body or a model house.

Whatever materials are used, children require plenty of time to practise techniques as focused activities (Dawes 1996). Very young children require practice with cutting skills. The notion of progressive development in using scissors was explored earlier. From the beginning, children should complete the necessary cutting in all their products. Ideally, children have materials that they can cut for themselves, but occasionally when a child wants to cut something such as thin tissue paper adult intervention may be necessary. If this situation does arise then children must be fully involved in working with the adult concerned. The aim is for the adult to model practice, in collaboration with the child, thus avoiding feelings of inadequacy. To enable progression to occur, provide under-fives with a table of scrap card that they may cut in any way they wish. As the teacher observes the children cutting, suggestions may be made to attempt a different cut. For example, a teacher observing a child to be proficient in cutting into the card several times (and giving task-specific praise) suggests cutting all the way across. This is the next challenge for the child. Introducing children to challenging their skills in this way is much less threatening than attempting to produce a perfect product without the practice. A target sheet as suggested in Chapter 4 is useful in this situation as it enables the children to be fully aware of their own progress in developing the skills. For very young children pictures will be more appropriate than words.

As suggested previously, progression links to the types of materials introduced. Thin card and stiff paper are much easier for children to work with than tissue paper when cutting with scissors or other cutters such as circular cutters. One can make sharp folds in paper more easily than in card. Card requires the use of a scoring tool such as a perforation cutter. Cutting around the outside of a piece of material is easier than cutting holes out of the centre. Children must learn appropriate techniques for cutting rectangular holes and the correct use of circular cutters. Using a large circular cutter in two hands is much easier for many children than the small cutters that operate like a pair of compasses in mathematics. For circular cutters, children should learn how to use a cutting board on which to fasten the paper or card with masking tape.

Folding skills require a similar opportunity to practise in a focused way. Beginning with under-fives again, provide plenty of scrap paper and card to allow the children to practise their folding techniques. Matching corner to corner and creating a sharp fold down a central line in the paper is a challenging task for many children. Cooperative opportunities arise here as one child may hold the corners in place while another creates the fold. Introducing a ruler or other instrument is unnecessary and serves to make the task more complex. The main idea that children must remember is to run the hand from the outer edges towards the fold and not the other way. These simple techniques require some direct teaching. Once children have learned to fold paper in half they may be challenged to fold it into quarters and eighths. They may progress to folding across diagonals, folding zigzags, and eventually creating a simple product such as an open box, or one of those 'fortune-telling' games that children enjoy. These are simple origami techniques. Once children are proficient in folding paper, then folding with card is a progression that requires the addition of a scoring tool.

Once children have learned to be proficient in specific techniques when making simple products, they may then incorporate those techniques into a design. Child Activity 16 uses the template designed in Child Activity 9 to create a box for a simple product. The template may be simply a collection of rectangular shapes. The children will have practised folding it to discover whether it will create a box. The next step is to decide how the edges will fit together when folded. Tabs are required and the children must discover through further modelling where to place these. A common error that children make is to add tabs to all sides. Masking tape is useful here because it creates a tab that also provides a temporary join. Some children will be ready to add a window to their template. They will develop the skills necessary to cut out such a window from paper and card through focused activities. The main methods to aid progression are:

- focused tasks to teach new skills;
- an opportunity to practise in an unthreatening environment;
- teacher intervention that encourages groups and individuals to progress their skills;
- clear target setting to enable children to be aware of progress;
- increasing the level of challenge within an activity as appropriate to the child and task.

Other flexible sheet materials such as heat-mouldable foam provide an opportunity for experience with materials not usually used within the classroom and in this sense provide progression through a broadening of specialist skill applicable to the material. Again, within the scope of the materials, there must be identifiable opportunities to challenge individual children to extend their knowledge, skills and understanding.

Child Activity 16 – All boxed up

Aim: To help individual children progress their skill in creating a box from card.

Resources:

- templates from Child Activity 9
- a selection of coloured card
- a selection of coloured paper, and other items to decorate a gift box
- scissors, perforation cutters, circular cutters, craft knives and safety rulers
- masking tape, PVA glue and spreaders
- acetate sheets.

Task:

From the response to Child Activity 9 identify children who require focused teaching to progress a particular skill, or to develop some knowledge and understanding.

(a) In what position are extra flaps useful on this net to allow the lid to close effectively? How will you help the children work this out on their?

(b) Some children may not have been able to plan for a window in the box lid. Identify the reasons for this and teach the children what they need to know to complete this challenge.

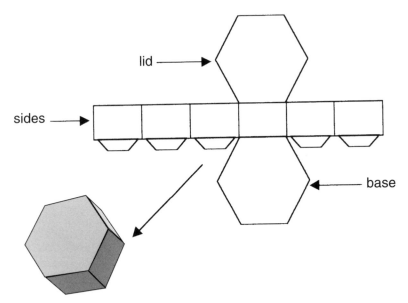

The children are to make the box for which they created a net in Child Activity 9.

Discussion points:

- What focused teaching did you provide?

- How did you cater for different needs?

- Did all children make progress?

- How can you identify the progress that individual children have made?

- Did any children set their own challenges to make the task more difficult?

Rigid sheet materials

Materials such as sheets of corrugated card or plastic provide another level of challenge. The focus changes from developing the application of cutting and folding skills to the specific techniques for cutting, shaping and joining such materials. Each material provides different working characteristics. Corrugated card, for example, is quite difficult for children to cut even with snips, while corrugated plastic may be easier. For the best effect, children will use a cutting knife and this has implications for safety in relation to the age of the children. Smaller pieces of rigid sheet material are easier to cut or shape than larger pieces. Similarly, sheet wood of various kinds will provide different opportunities to saw and shape, including the use of a shaper saw to cut holes and to cut curved edges to products.

Use of rigid sheet materials will mean that a framework is often unnecessary, as the supporting structure becomes the material itself. For example when making a model house, teachers of younger children are often tempted to use card from large boxes, with little consideration given to the difficulties children may have in cutting windows and doors. In many instances, a better way forward for younger children will be to learn how to make a frame from wood and attached flexible sheets to create the sides. The use of flexible sheet materials supported on an appropriate framework will produce a higher quality product. For Teacher Activity 20, however, the inclusion of both framework and rigid sheet materials is desirable.

Although skill development seems to have the main emphasis in the chapter so far, one cannot ignore the fact that children will be developing their knowledge of the materials, mechanisms and structures. This occurs through sound focused skill development and relevant tasks. Progression depends on the teacher's ability to provide effective learning situations through sound understanding of the subject and the ability to provide the next level of challenge (Whitfield in Foreword, NAAIDT 1998).

Framework materials

The notion of progression in the understanding of structures is a complex issue. The variables involved using different materials to create frameworks mean that one must look closely at the materials used, and the ways in which they connect to create structures. Initial experience of frameworks is often through use of various construction kits that have various struts and connectors. The use of construction kits will have a clearly progressive element if the nature of the kits is developmental throughout the school. Most producers of kits provide a variety suitable to different stages of learning that enable progressive steps to be easily identified. One of the dangers, however, is that some children fail to make progress if the children are limited to a particular kit designed for their age group when the next kit may be more suitable.

A typical example is the assumption that younger children require kits with larger pieces. Some younger children are very dextrous and have fine motor skills that will only be further developed through the use of kits with smaller pieces. All sizes should be available. Commercial kits in different sizes have interchangeable pieces. An accurate mathematical ratio is fundamental to their design. Kits allow children to explore challenging ideas at a younger age than previously expected. Five-year-old children may build models with simple gears and explore what happens when different sizes of wheel are used. The use of kits therefore encourages early understanding of some quite difficult concepts.

Wood and art straws seem to be the next two most popular materials. Art straws provide a comparatively cheap resource, but are often unsuitable for design-and-make tasks. The use of art straws as a construction material requires the teaching of specific techniques for joining, and from this point of view their use may be a valuable exercise. There is a progressive development in the specific techniques and the ways in which the children may employ these. If used in this way, then art straws may add to the broadening of the children's experiences. Art straws are particularly useful for modelling ideas before making products in expensive materials.

Wood is far more expensive and providing every class with experience in using wood to design and make a product results in a larger resource bill than many schools can afford. Some schools use offcuts of wood from a local joinery, but often these are unsuitable for the type of work children will do. Plastic struts for shaping and cutting are an alternative to wood but are also comparatively expensive.

For progression to occur in the use of any of these materials they need to be experienced regularly in school. Experiences of making with wood, for example, may follow the following broad progression:

1. sticking and nailing offcuts of wood together to make a toy;
2. using lollipop sticks to create a decorative effect on a model;
3. making a simple picture frame by gluing lollipop sticks together;
4. using junior hacksaw and bench hook to cut a piece of 1 cm dowel for a puppet stick;
5. using sandpaper to smooth rough edges;
6. using a junior hacksaw to cut four pieces of 1 cm-square wood to create a rectangular frame, with card joints, to display some weaving;
7. using a drill to create holes to make a ladder from rectangular wood and 6 mm dowel;
8. creating a three-dimensional framework for the walls of a model house using fixed joints appropriate to the task;
9. cutting mitre joints using a specialised jig as part of a pets' playground construction;
10. creating a three-dimensional construction that may be taken apart, and rebuilt.

Alongside this strand is a measuring and marking strand that broadly follows the child's mathematical development. This will range from 'measuring by eye', through measuring by comparison with a stick provided by the teacher, to the use of a range of non-standard and standard units.

The strands evident in the broad progression are:

- measuring skills and techniques – simple methods, larger units – choosing from a range of methods, tools and smaller units;
- cutting techniques – becoming more accurate and more specialised;

- fixing and strengthening techniques – simple to more complex;
- dimensions – mainly working from two dimensions to three dimensions.

Finishing techniques also feature in the form of learning how to smooth rough edges with sandpaper. Much more depth of thought is necessary in considering the use of various colouring and varnishing techniques also. The finish must be suited to the purpose of the product and not just the aesthetic value. It will be noted again that this is not an exhaustive list, nor is it strictly linear. The main purpose of attempting to identify strands is to become aware of the possibilities and opportunities with the materials so that teacher intervention provides for progressive development of these skills in making.

Quality

Values and beliefs inevitably influence judgements of quality. An adult's judgement of quality may be very different from that of a child. A child may put emphasis on all the hard work put into designing and making a product. The appearance might be the focus and often for very young children whether they like their own product is of all-consuming importance; an adult may look at the child's designing and making with a different focus. An adult may make normative comparisons and place more emphasis on whether the product meets the needs of the user. From a teacher's point of view it is most important to develop a shared understanding with the children about how to make judgements, suited to the capability of the children.

A simplistic approach explores quality in three broad strands through the Key Stages:

- craft quality;
- technical quality;
- fitness for purpose (Stein and Poole 1997).

In attempting to use these headings there is some difficulty in deciding where to categorise some aspects. They might also suggest that products have more importance than the process. More detailed thought must be given and more emphasis clearly on the processes. An alternative view of the strands of quality may be:

- quality of process;
- quality of product;
- quality through progression (NAAIDT 1998).

The notion of quality through progression is fundamental to design and technology. The main reason for making progress is to improve quality through the application of improved skills, knowledge and understanding. The process children work through is as important as the product because it is only by improving processes in the classroom that children will move towards quality products. Improved decision-making and the ability to justify ideas evidence improving processes. Children will become more able to plan their projects in a logical way, and will rigorously test their ideas. In relation to products, the aim is to ensure that the product is successful and meets the design specification. The children will make efficient use of materials and have an acceptable standard of finish. There will be evidence of increasing awareness of aesthetic, social,

Figure 3.8 A mask by a seven-year-old

moral and cultural values in their work. Quality in progression will arise through consolidation of knowledge and understanding, together with increasing confidence in applying this to practical design-and-make tasks.

Let us consider the process a child of seven worked through independently and identify some quality issues that arise. The child designed and made a mask to wear at a Halloween party. The character decided upon was the witch's cat. The design is in Figure 3.8 and the mask was made from card off a cereal box.

The child followed the design closely, as can be seen in the photograph. Throughout the process, there was constant consideration of size, position and shape. The position of the eyeholes was determined by looking in a mirror and marking the spot with a finger. The child asked for help in cutting out holes and was successful with the demonstrated technique. Whiskers came from the backing paper of double-sided sticky tape, making good use of the limited resources available. The child used skills appropriate to the task, and at a level expected for the age group. The resulting mask painted only on the plain side of the card is of good quality and serves the purpose well for that child. However, there is room for further development of the child's thinking about quality in terms of both process and product:

- Perhaps the design drawing could have annotations that require the child to plan more carefully (improving quality of process).
- If the mask was for another, the child might think of providing a better finish to both sides of the mask (improving quality of product).

- Better quality card might make a better quality product.
- Evaluation of existing products before making might have provided the incentive to work in three dimensions.
- Teaching of focused skills to use card or paper for three-dimensional structures will encourage the child to use them on the mask.

The list comprises a few suggestions, and there could be others. The purpose in looking at the task with a view to improving quality is to demonstrate that issues of quality in design and technology are also issues of effective teaching. The teacher in this case adopted a non-interventionist role in order to observe the result. Taking time to observe is as important as teaching because observations inform the teacher how and when interventions will improve the quality without taking away the child's creativity. If teachers learn how and when to intervene then teaching is more effective in terms of improving quality of progression.

The activity also highlights the difference between a child's level of quality and an adult's. It would be too easy to take over and tell the child what to do, rather than providing appropriate situations or suitable interventions that challenge a child to rethink and modify to improve quality. To encourage children to think in more depth about quality of product they must begin to make products for others, and not just themselves; their evaluations are the key to improving quality. Children's evaluations may take on a subtle difference when they begin to think about someone else using their product.

Developing skills of evaluation has an important role in helping a child's design and technology capability to progress. Evaluation of existing products raises awareness of the possibilities, the materials and processes used, function and fitness for purpose. It encourages children to consider the values inherent in the making and marketing of products which will then affect the way materials are used in their own. Looking at products gives children insights into their function and the knowledge gained is directly applicable to the task of designing and making a similar product (Bowen 1995). Bowen provides a comprehensive list of questions that encourage a focus on the following aspects:

- form, e.g. what does it look/feel/smell/sound like?
- construction, e.g. how was it made?
- function, e.g. how well does it work?
- context, e.g. how does it affect the environment?
- future predictions, e.g. could it be improved?

Many of the questions focus on quality issues and encourage both breadth and depth of thought. Working in this way with existing products will develop skills of evaluation that will transfer into situations where the children evaluate their own products.

Children will naturally evaluate their own work, but will not necessarily articulate the evaluation and the teacher has an important role in encouraging such communication (Constable 1994c). Evaluating involves considering the weak points as well as the strengths; it is an ongoing process throughout the task. Improving the skill of evaluation is dependent upon the teacher intervening at appropriate times to ask the challenging question, and to provoke thought. Good intervention helps to maintain confidence and prevents children from following unsound procedures that may ruin the outcome entirely. Younger children often cannot find fault with their work while older children are more often able to describe problems that arose during the process and the difficulties they had. Young children will often discard an idea that they find too difficult to put into practice, while an older child might take a risk and try something out. The teacher's task is to try to draw out the issues while the child is working on the project. For younger pupils some encouragement to think ahead and to consider what they may find difficult will enable the teacher to provide the necessary teaching to help the children overcome the difficulties.

More effective working develops from children's evaluation of their own process. The aim should be to become more systematic and to be able to develop a clear plan. From an initial broad range of ideas, children must learn how to develop a clear design proposal. The ability to identify strengths and weaknesses in designs will only come through opportunities to share and communicate with others. Thus, the teacher should provide opportunities for peer review alongside self-evaluation. To be able to develop clear design plans children need sound knowledge of the materials and processes involved.

As children move through the school their knowledge of materials should broaden and deepen. The idea that decisions sometimes have to be made to focus on ensuring progression in the use of one material, i.e. depth, rather than provide a range of materials at the same level, i.e. breadth, is introduced in Chapter 4. Schools must maintain a balance.

Quality is not just about the product: it is about the whole process of teaching and learning design and technology. Quality is broadly age-related, and experience-related, so judgements of quality made by the teacher must be within the bounds of the activity, the child's capability and the quality of the learning experience. An essential question to ask when children do not produce the expected quality of product is whether the process has been high quality in relation to the classroom provision. Poor quality tools and materials, and poor quality teaching will result in poor quality products. If the level of challenge is too high then the quality is likely to be low because of the children's lack of knowledge or skill. With a level of challenge too low, the quality may still be low because the children think that the teacher is expecting little of them. The most difficult task for the teacher is to ensure that the level of challenge is just right for all children to ensure quality in all aspects. To focus attention on quality Teacher Activity 17 uses the mock-up from Teacher Activity 11 as a template for making a vehicle body from card. The idea of target setting as a means for developing quality in progression has a section in Chapter 4.

Teacher Activity 17 – A quality dream car

Aim: To develop an understanding of the issues affecting quality in the design-and-make process.

Resources:

• the dream car template made in Teacher Activity 11

Figure 3.9 The net produced from Figure 2.16

• card
• scissors
• PVA glue and glue sticks
• masking tape
• various graphical media
• clear acetate
• scoring tools
• cutting knives, safety rulers and boards
• the chassis from Teacher Activity 11.

Task: As a professional designer you must present your design ideas, including a realistic model of the 'dream car', to the managing directors of Designer Vehicles Inc.

1. Review and evaluate your initial sketches and the mock-up. Develop a template from the mock-up and create the model vehicle body from card. The model vehicle must have a demonstration opening door and a clear indication of specific external features that make the design unique.
2. Prepare a short presentation in which you justify your design to the panel of directors.

Evaluation:

• Reflect on the quality of the process and product – e.g. consider clarity of design specification, planning, justification, use of materials, quality of joins, consideration of aesthetics and function, understanding of the materials and processes involved, application of knowledge, communication skills.
• What implications are there for developing a shared understanding of 'quality' with children?

Chapter 4

Moving Forward

Teacher assessment

This section focuses on formative assessment processes before looking at planning. Assessment of open-ended practical activities is more complex than assessment of clearly focused and structured activities, simply because of the range of outcomes. It therefore follows that the teacher requires secure knowledge and understanding of various directions in which a child may take the project. The management of such assessments requires thought and forward planning, and becomes easier by involving the children in the process. If children are fully aware of their own targets for learning then they will be able to assess their own progress in collaboration with the teacher. Forward planning and involvement of the pupils ensures that clear targets are set for learning objectives.

First consideration is to the strands for assessment in design and technology. This book centres on progression in teaching skills, knowledge and understanding of design and technology. Capability is something that encompasses all of these things. If we teach these strands then a means of assessing them has to be established. Different writers on the subject have slightly different views, so first a look at the suggestions. The Assessment of Performance Unit model of design and technology as the interaction of mind and hand suggests assessment in the following strands:

- conceptual understanding (mind);
- communicative/modelling facility (hand);
- interaction between the two (APU 1994).

One of the difficulties with the literature is that the terminology used varies, and for the classroom practitioner there is little practical guidance, but when the terminology is examined commonalities exist. For example, interaction between conceptual understanding and communicative modelling facility results in what many will identify as capability. Another approach might be to look at projects that children undertake from two different viewpoints:

- a holistic view of how the child handles the whole project;
- a focused view of particular aspects (Doherty *et al.* 1994).

The holistic view will inevitably include the interaction between mind and hand as part of the process, while the particular aspects may focus on the conceptual understanding, practical skills or knowledge. Neither model specifically includes knowledge as a distinct strand from understanding, nor do the models facilitate assessment in practice. From a primary school perspective it is easier to look at assessment of a design-and-make task in three clear strands, all of which may include some conceptual, communicative and modelling skills. The three strands are:

1. Designing skills, e.g.
   - using sources of information;
   - drawing;
   - planning;
   - evaluating.

2. Making skills, e.g.
   - selecting appropriate materials;
   - measuring;
   - joining;
   - finishing techniques;
   - evaluation.

3. Knowledge and understanding, e.g.
   - how simple mechanisms work;
   - how structures fail;
   - how simple products function;
   - fitness for purpose;
   - recognition of hazards;
   - appropriate vocabulary (DfE 1995).

Within a lesson there may be a focused activity to emphasise the development of one strand. For example, evaluating existing products will emphasise the application of knowledge and understanding, while focused teaching of the use of a drill clearly emphasises making skills. Later in this chapter there is a section on planning that will encourage assessment of these three strands.

The assessment of values, beliefs and attitudes appears to have been ignored, but as these inevitably influence all aspects of a design-and-make task then it is difficult to make a specific assessment for them alone. When a child considers a product's fitness for purpose the decisions reflect values held by the child. For example, on examination of a plastic toy car designed for a toddler, one child may suggest that wood is a better material because it takes less energy to produce, and is a product that will not pollute. Another child might suggest that the use of plastic is acceptable in this particular product because it is safe and strong while wood is chewable. Both provide sound points and hold generally acceptable values in relation to the issues raised. Therefore the difficulties arise in deciding which values demonstrate progression. The teacher's own values, beliefs and attitudes will influence judgements made. Instead of focusing on the values, it is better to focus on whether children are developing the ability to apply their growing knowledge and understanding of a range of issues to a situation.

Similarly, in assessing capability the teacher has to take the holistic approach, but later, when discussing planning, issues arise about the effects of context on capability. It may be that a child performs well in one context and not in another. Formative assessments of process and product are essential to the whole process of ensuring progression and developing quality. The key to successful assessment is to give children clear objectives so that they are fully engaged in improving their own practice. Plans will identify these objectives and possible assessment methods. Teachers will also need to know exactly what to look for in the process and in the product that will help them to establish whether a child has achieved the objectives. Some aspects of design and technology are relatively easy to assess. For example, if a child has two targets:

1. be able to cut along a straight line with a pair of scissors;
2. evaluate products with the user in mind;

for the first, the child will be able to identify the success by the outcome, but to discover whether a child has achieved the second target, the teacher will have to ask questions and encourage the child to communicate the evaluation. Both targets are easier to assess when the child has clear knowledge of them, and will therefore aim to develop those specific skills.

Teacher Activity 18 focuses on target setting for individual children. The use of target sheets may begin with the same targets for the whole class. As different children begin to show particular achievements their targets will become more focused to their individual development. Conversely, other children will require the same target in several different contexts for successful achievement. Some scheme materials provide such sheets as a record sheet, with a generic list of skills that a child will gain from a unit of work. Often the teacher will record that a child has experienced the activity, and will sometimes make an assessment of it. Target sheets are not purely record sheets because the intention is for the teacher and child to use them as a formative process. They may list only the skill, knowledge and understanding that require development for a particular child or group; they will not necessarily list every possible line of progression within a project. Target sheets are primarily for identifying specific progressive steps for individuals or groups. Thus, we can move away from just thinking about the progression inherent in the activity, and turn thoughts to the progressive development of the individual child.

The aim is for the children to have awareness of their development. The children will become aware that they make progress through working on those aspects in which they lack skill, knowledge or understanding. Through using such sheets children become more aware of the need to demonstrate their capabilities to others. In this way, the child is performing a self-assessment. The targets for a class, group or individual will reflect your knowledge of their capabilities and their previous experiences. The targets set during planning become the assessment records so the whole process is integrated. With children fully aware of their own development, the burden on the teacher reduces.

Now look back at Teacher/Child Activity 3, in which the challenge was to produce

Teacher Activity 18 – Target setting for progression

Aim: To consider the use of targets for individual children to identify their goals.

Task:

Look at the example target sheets below and consider how they are part of a progression.

- What may the child have achieved before, and what is the next step?
- What possibilities exist for splitting targets into smaller steps?
- What are the possibilities for encouraging children to identify their own targets to aid progression?

Example target sheet for children to use

Name: _____ Age: _____ Class: _____

Date: _____ Activity: *Making a pop-up card*

Skill/knowledge/understanding	Comment
Understand the design brief	
Develop evaluation criteria that consider the user	
Produce an outline plan of the project	

Skill/knowledge/understanding	Comment
Produce accurately measured three-dimensional design drawings	
Use a series of platform mechanisms to create the card	
Model ideas in scrap paper before making	
Produce clear lettering	
Use scissors to cut detailed outlines	
Use glue sparingly to achieve a good bond	
Evaluate the process	

different types of pop-up mechanisms and consider how this challenge approach may fit in with the target setting sheet. The challenge may be one of the initial targets or alternatively sheets designed with extra spaces for extra challenges as required. Figures 4.1 and 4.2 show the results of two different challenges. Perhaps you will recognise the challenge that stimulated Figure 4.1. The other challenge was different: it challenged the children to modify the platform so that it was a different shape. The results can be fascinating and such a challenge provided for creative exploration of ideas through modelling.

For a child of seven the challenge was to use the simple platform and create a birthday card for a friend. Before making, the child had experience in folding paper and cutting simple platforms but she had not made such a card before. She then explained all the features that would go on such a card, and proceeded to make a hat to stick on the platform. Trial and error was the method for making and modifying the hat. Thought about clear lettering and other suitable design features is also evident. At no point did the child try to draw a design. The design was drawn, modelled and modified as part of the final product, except for practising the lettering for the card when an adult helped with spelling. Figure 4.3 shows the resulting card interior. The child did not consider the exterior features of the card, perhaps because of the way the challenge had been set. The teacher's role now is to consider how the child went through the process and plan for further development. What might this child be challenged to do next? What specific targets are useful to aid progression? It might be useful to reflect on this before attempting Teacher Activity 19.

Teacher Activity 19 is an opportunity to create a target sheet for a group of children or the class. It has to be for a specific project. Schools may usefully link this activity to Teacher Activity 20 later in the chapter. The blank form provides space for up to ten targets. All the spaces do not have to be in use, nor is there a need to include every aspect the children will learn. Include those for which exploration of the children's understanding will be most useful, and those known to be a progressive development for them. The use of information technology to produce such a sheet aids modification of the list in the light of experience. If convenient, the electronic storage of the whole record is possible, but hard copy is useful for the child to keep as part of their portfolio for a project. The sheet is for joint use with the children to discover what they feel

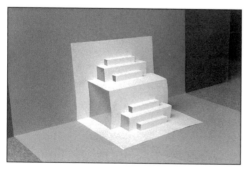

Figure 4.1 Platforms within platforms

Figure 4.2 A star-shaped platform

Figure 4.3 A pop-up birthday card – by Jenny (age seven)

capable of doing. Complete the activity, ensuring that the children focus their attention on the list. The children will aim to develop the skills, knowledge and understanding identified. You will aim to teach them what they need to know.

To help to evaluate the children's responses the following questions are useful:

- Do all the children feel confident about the same things?
- Can the children identify their achievements or do they need adult help?
- Is the sheet a useful part of the process?
- Does it help the teacher?
- Does it help the learner to make progress?
- Will the children be able to help the teacher clarify the next set of targets?

It seems that the focus here is on providing a record, but the developing process is much more important. Figure 4.4 shows the lines of thought. It is clear that children are fully involved in the whole process under the guidance of the teacher. A more effective learning situation develops, as each child becomes more aware of the necessary progress to target. Once the system is in place it is self-sustaining and transferable across the whole school.

The target sheet provides a clear record, alongside other evidence gathered in a child's portfolio. Written comments from the teacher on the child's work provide evidence of judgements made, e.g. 'This design is excellent and shows that you can now draw in perspective'.

Teacher Activity 19 – Target setting 2

Aim: To develop the skill of target setting.

Task:

1. Create your own set of targets for a group of children or the class. The targets will be for a specific project of your choice. Use the blank form that provides space for up to six items.
2. Use the checklist and evaluate the response of the children.

Name: _____ Age: _____ Class: _____

Date: _____ Activity: _____

Skill, knowledge, understanding	Comment

Children too can keep photographs and process diaries that provide evidence of their achievements. Process diaries will provide space for the recording of thoughts and feelings as well as the factual records of process (Bratt and Djora 1995). Children can feel free to make comment on their own achievements. Thus a holistic record develops. For younger children teachers might use a sticker system that highlights achievements and celebrates success. Some schools have software packages to enable them to design their own stickers (see Figure 4.5).

Imaginative use of such comments that celebrate achievements provides a record of assessment that reflects classroom practice and avoids the assessment record becoming a chore. The process of assessment integrates with the process of planning. Thorough planning and full involvement of the children provide smooth running formative assessment processes.

Planning for progression

The previous section had a clear focus on planning for individual children's targets to aid assessment procedures with the aim of improving the quality of progression. It is necessary for a whole school to use the progression within the subject as a basis for planning decisions. This broad progression then allows the teacher to establish classroom practice allowing a focus on individual progression. This section will focus on some of the broader whole-school issues related to progression.

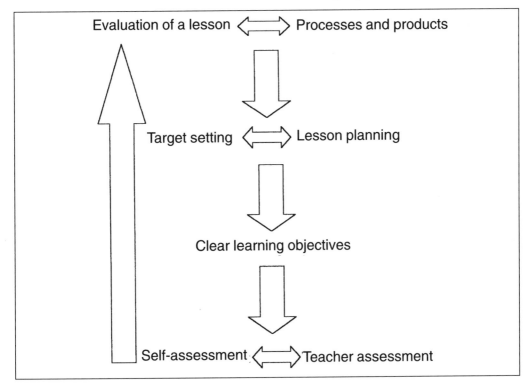

Figure 4.4 Formative assessment through target setting

Figure 4.5 Examples of stickers

A primary school is required to provide a broad and balanced curriculum. Design and technology is a subject that helps to fulfil the requirement for a broad curriculum because it draws on many other subject areas. In planning for coverage of design and technology, a school must be aware of the dangers of a piecemeal approach in attempting to teach all aspects. It may be better to follow a few lines of progression through the school thoroughly than to attempt to provide a broad experience base with limited progression. Schools therefore have choices to make about:

- the types of materials they can best utilise;
- the amount of time they will allocate to the subject;
- the length of time slots on the timetable;
- opportunities for children to revisit specific aspects, enabling progression of skills, knowledge and understanding.

This may mean identifying aspects that are ongoing in a variety of ways. For example, use of scissors occurs in other subject areas for all kinds of purposes. A school may choose to ensure that there is a sound progression in the skill of using scissors regardless of the design and technology taught. There will also be specific aspects of the subject to teach in blocks of time, perhaps as a topic. Allocation of topics to age groups with provision made for revisiting the topic at another level of understanding allows for progression. The main difficulty is ensuring that the experiences are meaningful and provide for sound progressive development.

A scheme of work may include a unit of work with fabric at age eight and age ten. In these circumstances, these two units are less likely to provide for progressive development in textile skills than if the children use textiles every year. Three options are available to schools:

1. Choose three very different materials, e.g. flexible sheet materials, textiles and wood. Provide experiences to enable clear progressive development with these materials in each school year.

The advantage of such an approach is that the school can provide for clear progressive steps of development. The staff will know and understand the chosen materials well. The option provides for clear development of process skills. On transfer to secondary school, the primary school will be able to identify the materials and tools used, and the nature of the children's experiences. The disadvantage is that children will not experience some materials at all, unless they fit into other subjects, e.g. experiences with food through scientific activities.

2. Provide a range of topics in which there is flexible use of a range of materials and focus on developing the design-and-make process skills in a holistic way.

The advantage here is that the children will use a range of materials and processes, but not necessarily in a coherent way. They may make good progress in the generic aspects of problem-solving, but progression in children's ability to apply skills, knowledge and understanding to a situation is often context-dependent; a child that completes an excellent project with card may not repeat such excellence with wood. Progression is thus difficult to identify clearly. The secondary school will not have a clear idea of the children's skill, knowledge and understanding with particular materials.

3. Create a two-year rolling programme that provides experience of all materials and process skills, with the opportunity to make progress with specific materials every alternate year.

This is a common approach when attempting to provide experience of every possible material and process. It does provide for some progression but in a more limited way than if the children experience the use of a particular material each year. The advantage is that children gain a broad experience that will provide a baseline for further study at secondary school.

There are also some benefits to making use of other subject lessons for developing design and technology skills or vice versa. For example, science lessons may include observational drawing, while in art there will be opportunities to work on perspective drawing as a specific skill. Alternatively, the design and technology lesson is a relevant opportunity to focus on the mathematics of two-dimensional and three-dimensional relationships. The creation of nets to make gift boxes, houses or vehicle bodies is much more interesting than working on nets in a pure mathematical exercise. However, design and technology ought not to link with a specific subject such as art all the time, or the distinctive qualities of the subject are lost. The danger is that the activities become craft activities rather than engaging children in the full process. Schools must consider these issues. A rigid timetable might not allow for coherence in following a project through. On the other hand, it is good for children to return to and rethink projects on a regular basis. Sometimes a longer block of time is beneficial, and allows children to follow a project through from start to finish. Flexibility is important.

Some materials do exist that help the teacher focus on the detailed progression within specific aspects of the subject. Guidance on implementing the subject provides examples of how a particular strand developed (NCC 1991). Specialist organisations have produced charts and tables related to the development of their own subject area (National Association of Teachers of Home Economics (NATHE) 1994). Similarly, many local education authorities have produced schemes for schools to follow. Schools have the opportunity to draw on the available resources to create their own scheme that provides clearly for progression.

Whatever programme ensues, progression is assured by planning clearly stated design-and-make tasks. These must be appropriate to the ability, the interests and the experiences of pupils, and must fit into a clearly assessable programme of work (NAAIDT 1998). The danger in following the broad planning approach is that conceptual lines of progression are lost. Often the focus is on what the children will make rather than on conceptual development: both require some thought in the broad plan. If children use textiles at six, eight and ten, then decisions are necessary about the expected level of conceptual development through the nature of the challenge posed. As children mature one may expect them to apply their knowledge, skills and values in a more focused manner than younger children. Progression is the ability to handle individual concepts with increasing breadth and depth as well as handling a larger number of increasingly complex concepts (Doherty *et al.* 1994). An example follows.

Possible textile units in a scheme:

- Age six – design and make a bookmark using Binca and embroidery thread.
- Age eight – investigate a range of shoe bags to list their qualities. Design and make a personalised shoe bag from a basic pattern, using fabric crayons or felt collage to create the design.
- Age ten – research literature about protective clothing. Visit a food outlet to observe protective clothing in use and consider its purpose. Design and make an apron.

The first activity at age six focuses on the designing and making skills with large needles and very open weave fabric. The second at age eight includes development of knowledge through evaluation of existing products, and these inform the making process with finer needles and closer weave fabric. It also moves into three dimensions, producing a structure that will hold an item and that will close with a draw string mechanism. The project is comparatively simple as the children will use the same rectangular pattern, but they will personalise the design. The final project at age ten includes researching literature and looking beyond personal requirements to the needs of industry and the public. It includes specific health and safety issues. The product is more challenging than the shoe bag because the children have to shape the fabric and consider a range of finishing techniques and fastenings. Each project is therefore conceptually more demanding than the previous one. However, the approach may also be criticised in that it does not allow for smaller steps of development between them. To address this problem a teacher may use records of previous achievements to set targets for the children at appropriate levels. Thus a child that had difficulty in sewing on Binca at age six, may prefer to sew a shoe bag with a more open weave fabric than another child, thus allowing for the use of a larger needle. A child who shows great proficiency in the use of a needle at six may be encouraged to develop a more complex design using some embroidery stitches on the shoe bag. The broad progression provided by the scheme thus allows for an individual focus at classroom level.

Although focusing on designing skills, making skills and knowledge simplifies the planning and assessing process, there is also a need to retain a broader picture of a child's capability. Capability in design and technology encompasses both skills and knowledge. It is the ability to apply knowledge and skills to the problem-solving situation. Design and technology is split into the following categories:

- procedural skills, i.e. designing and making skills;
- knowledge and understanding;
- practical capability (Johnsey 1997).

Practical capability is an aspect unique to the subject, and as previously mentioned in Chapter 1 relates to the child's level of maturity as well as their experience. It follows that the more experience a child has, the more likely they are to achieve capability. Thus, the implications for the whole-school planning are that children require regular experiences to achieve capability. However, the notion is not helpful to a school in deciding exactly which balance of experiences to provide, i.e. whether to use a broad or narrow selection of materials and processes. The broad selection may provide for progressive development of capability in a generic problem-solving sense perhaps. The narrower, in depth focus on materials may allow for greater demonstration of capability with those specific materials, e.g. as shown by a joiner in designing and making window frames or by a cook in developing a new dish. The question is whether we want our primary school children to become specialists in a few materials or generalists in terms of the problem-solving approach. Both directions have their merits. Most important is to recognise that capability is assessed by the holistic approach of looking at how the child applies skill, knowledge and understanding to the design-and-make task.

Even more importantly, in relation to teaching and assessing the subject, the teacher must allow children to take a flexible route through the procedures. Children may begin the design-and-make process using any of the skills, and for young children making has more emphasis than designing (Johnsey 1997). In the classroom the assessment must not rest on whether the child designs on paper, for example, before making. However, the implications for planning require thought. If designing is not assumed to precede making then a teacher planning for a series of lessons may adopt a more open-ended approach in which children follow their own process. The alternative is to structure the lesson to cater for a specific expected development. Both approaches may be acceptable in different circumstances aiming to develop different aspects of the subject. If the development of specific skills or knowledge is the aim of a particular lesson then a focused approach is best. If the aim is the development of capability in application of the subject skills, knowledge and understanding then the open-ended approach is best.

Most design-and-make tasks in school will require a mixed approach in which some aspects are taught to the children as focused tasks followed by an open-ended approach. The aim of the open-ended task is to incorporate some of the newly learned skills, knowledge or understanding. Targets set during the planning phase will reflect the range of aspects, and, particularly with older children, may become part of the planning element of their project. If their capability is developing well then children will begin to identify how they can improve on their previous efforts through setting their own targets.

Teacher Activity 20 brings the focus back to the specific classroom situation to identify specific learning objectives for a series of lessons. Two sheets provide some guidance through the process. The suggested activity is 'the pet's playground', but any similar activity will substitute. Use of the children's target setting sheet (Teacher Activity 19) usefully complements the process. The purpose of the activity is to explore the detailed thinking that underlies decisions made when planning a series of lessons on a theme. After teaching, the lessons reflect on the points suggested for group discussion, before moving on to consider differentiation.

Planning for differentiation

Chapter 1 provided a brief section on the issue of differentiation within the subject. Differentiation is essential for individual progression, but need not necessarily mean that particular children identified as having special needs in other areas of the curriculum are those who require specialist differentiation in design and technology. If a child has difficulties with language then it seems logical to assume that similar difficulties will affect communicative aspects of the design and technology process. However it is also too easy to assume that such children have little understanding of the processes simply because they cannot express them as coherently as another child. The development of a technical language is important too, but a child having difficulty with some of the language may still understand the concepts. The teacher's role is to ensure sound development of the necessary language skills through meaningful activities. In fact, design and technology may provide the motivation for the child to improve and develop communication skills. This motivation will often transfer to other subject areas.

Another difficulty is associated with mathematics and problems with measuring skills. Some children have poor spatial awareness and this affects their work in art, design and technology, physical education and mathematics. They may produce untidy work and seem unable to use measuring instruments accurately. Again, although the difficulty affects the design process and products the children are often very aware of

Teacher Activity 20 – Planning for progression: a pet's playground 2

Aim: To prepare in more detail for progression of specific skills, knowledge and understanding.

Resources:

- selected framework materials, e.g. wood, plastic rods and sheets
- PVA glue, glue-sticks and masking tape
- cutting tools appropriate for the materials
- plain and square paper for developing designs.

Task:

Plan and teach a series of 2–3 lessons in which the children complete the process of designing and making a pet's playground. They will work in teams to produce a group of separate items or a connected adventure playground, depending on their age and level of capability. The materials used may be any suitable framework or stiff sheet materials.

1. Plan to introduce the activity at an appropriate level for the children, based on your knowledge of their previous lessons. Write a brief summary here:

2. Consider the skills, knowledge and understanding that particular children need to develop. Identify particular elements of progression to work on with a small group.

3. Decide how to place the children in teams.
(a) You may decide that children at a similar skill level may work together. What may be the merits of this organisation?

(b) Alternatively, you may decide to work with the children in teams that reflect various strengths. How will working with such teams be different from (a)?

4. What knowledge will the children gain?

5. What focused tasks do you need to provide?

6. How will you organise the lessons to provide for them?

7. Children should be evaluating their product development throughout the whole process. How will your role support this?

Discussion points:

- Did the group of children make progress in the particular elements you identified for progression in Question 2?
- In what ways did your classroom organisation help to ensure progression?
- In what ways did it hinder development?
- In which elements of the curriculum did the whole class make progress?
- Which elements were progressed by specific groups or individuals?
- How did your role affect the children's progress?
- What did you do that was most helpful?

the issues surrounding quality. Their evaluations are often very honest, and they despair that they will ever be able to make anything that is better quality than their peers. Too often, these children opt out of the subject because they suffer disappointment and lack of self-esteem. The target setting approach can help such children because one can tailor the targets to ensure small progressive steps to enable success within each project. Instead of focusing on the comparative nature of evaluation alongside peers, children may evaluate their progress against previous achievements.

One cannot generalise about how to differentiate, and it is not within the scope of this book to look at specific cases. Instead, a few issues are raised to consider that will apply in any situation where a child requires individual attention to enable progression. That can apply to any child, at a particular time. Four different aspects of a child's learning may require consideration in the quest to provide suitably differentiated tasks:

1. the stimulus – and whether it is appropriate for all children;
2. the materials, tools and processes used in the activity;
3. the task and the way it is set, e.g. more open or more focused;
4. the possible outcomes and their purpose.

In most cases, the broad stimulus used to generate ideas with a class will be suitable for the class, but the specific focus that children look at may be different. To illustrate the point we can consider a visit to a supermarket. Some children may have the conceptual understanding to be able to look closely at health and safety issues from the point of view of the customer. Others may only be able to consider such issues from their own point of view. Any design-and-make tasks developing from this visit will reflect those conceptual differences, while the skill level expected in designing and making may be the same. Alternatively, the presentation of a task to one group of children might necessarily need to be more focused (Curriculum Council for Wales (CCW) 1994). The children complete the same task presented in different ways, thus altering the level of challenge. Earlier in the chapter the idea was raised of challenging children to work at different levels using different fabrics. The idea of presenting the activities as different challenges fits well with consideration of the types of materials and the way tasks are set. To be able to work in this way one requires knowledge of the range of possible outcomes.

For the teacher the concern is one of planning to meet different needs within the classroom. All planning stems from assessment of individual needs, and with the target setting approach the process is easier. Trainee teachers, in particular, have difficulty in planning for differentiation and too often plan to differentiate by outcome. In design and technology this may mean that some children feel as though they have failed because their product is not what they expected it to be. Planning to differentiate, if nothing else, should provide for all children to have a measure of success, so differentiation by outcome is insufficient in most cases.

Another popular way of differentiating is to provide more help to those who need it. Again, this can lead to the children involved feeling inadequate as they are set a task that perhaps has too high a level of challenge. Of course, setting them a different task may lead to low self-esteem too, so whatever provision is made it has to be planned so that the children know their individual strengths and weaknesses and have targeted for improvements. The key to success may be to set challenges in an open-ended way, allowing children to choose the level at which they work. This requires children to have sound knowledge of their own strengths and weaknesses discovered through clear target setting and evaluation.

What is clear is that planning for differentiation has to begin with the learning objectives, and the planning sheet identified as Teacher Activity 21 is designed as a training format that ensures a focus on differentiation. Working through the sheet for a particular topic first identifies the learning objectives. The headings of designing, making and knowledge encompass conceptual development, values, beliefs and attitudes. For any class there will be some children, or one child, who will have slightly different learning objectives in any one of these aspects. It might be a child who has exceptional skill in design drawing and who is ready to learn how to use isometric paper to develop more accuracy in three dimensions. During any scheme covering a few lessons there will be some focused tasks. Again, some children might not require the same focus as others. For example, children with language difficulties might benefit from plenty of oral work with an adult evaluating existing products while other children in the same class might work more independently before sharing ideas with the rest of the class. In each of the three strands identified there will be children that require specific teaching or a different approach to the task. These may be different children in different sections. One of the problems in many classrooms is the assumption that the same children always require extra help. Conversely, there is the assumption that the same children will always be successful. To ensure progression differentiated needs must show in planning at this specific level. The training format is interesting to work through while planning for a known class. It helps to identify how much or how little we know about individual children. If the target setting approach is established the format is easier to use. If not, then teachers must think very carefully about the achievements of each child, or at least groups of children, before making decisions about differentiation. Much differentiation occurs while 'on your feet' in the classroom as the teacher reacts to the children's responses to the task. However, until a teacher has thought through the implications of the plans for all the children she cannot begin to 'think on her feet' about individuals. The notion of the 'reflective practitioner' is an important one here. In design and technology, as in any subject, it is important to reflect on practice in order to make it more effective.

The final activity provides an opportunity to consider how to use information to inform planning for a new class. Teacher Activity 22 provides a scenario describing a Year 3 class that demonstrates a range of different skills, knowledge and under-standing. The aim of the exercise is to fine-tune the ability to use such information and identify needs and the teacher may also complete the activity using information from a particular class in school, but initially it is useful to work as a group on the same information and compare notes afterwards.

Combined with the scheme-planning format in Teacher Activity 21 it makes a useful simulated planning exercise. It is noticeable that knowing exactly what the children understand is difficult to identify from such information as it mainly focuses on skills

Teacher Activity 21 – Planning for differentiation

Outline scheme of work for design and technology Time-scale: weeks Class:	
Context/stimulus for project:	
Learning objectives for: Designing: Making: Knowledge:	Differentiation:
Cross-curricular links:	

Content	Organisation	Teacher action	Assessment criteria
Focused task(s):			
Differentiation:			

Content	Organisation	Teacher action	Assessment criteria
Designing:			
Differentiation:			
Making:			
Differentiation:			
Knowledge and understanding:			
Differentiation:			

Teacher Activity 22 – Identifying needs for a new class

Aim: To be able to use information about a class to help you identify possible targets for progression within a topic, and to plan a differentiated approach to teaching design and technology.

Task: Read the following scenario.

1. List the skills, knowledge and understanding that are identifiable from the information given.
2. Identify the possible progression that may occur in the next project for most children.
3. List the strengths and weaknesses of the five children that experience communication difficulties.
4. Identify any specific differentiation that is required, including making use of individual strengths.

Class scenario – Year 3

This class of 33 children has experienced a broad range of design-and-make activities. They have used a range of materials, including construction kits and off-cuts of wood from the local joinery. Most of their work is with paper, card and a range of 'found' materials. Outcomes are not always high quality because of the limitations of the materials used.

All except five children in the class demonstrate the ability to draw on their own experiences and to clarify ideas through discussion. Most produce detailed design drawings usually labelled to identify the various parts, but not always identifying materials and fixing techniques. Some children use their design drawings very closely to inform their making. They have all experienced creating 'mock-ups' from paper before making products in card. Through these experiences, they are developing skills of evaluation as part of the design process. All the children have experienced using a saw at least once, and most are competent with scissors. None has used a drill. They have experienced using Blu-tak and masking tape for temporary joins, and PVA glue for permanent joins. They are usually provided with materials and tools so they do not have to make choices about suitability of materials and tools as part of the process.

Five children experience great difficulty in communicating their ideas by any means and receive specialist support to develop their linguistic skills. Their design drawing skills vary, with one of the children in this group demonstrating exceptional skill in 3D sketching, while the other four show limited development through poor fine-motor control. In making products, these four children demonstrate much the same level of capability as the rest of the class unless fine control of scissors is required. All five are less able than most in making evaluative comments in relation to the purpose of the product.

and experiences. This emphasises the usefulness of the targeting approach that provides individual children's records showing progressive development across several aspects in a year. Some possibilities for progression are:

- the introduction of new materials, e.g. fabric;
- developing a more structured approach to using wood;
- improving the quality of outcomes by supplying appropriate choices of materials;
- developing planning skills, including more thought about materials and fixing techniques;
- encouraging all children to use their design drawings.

Specific differentiation will include encouraging the child who shows skill in three-dimensional sketching to develop more awareness of perspective and to help peers to begin to work more in three dimensions. The four children with particularly poor motor control can have focused tasks to improve their use of the pencil, e.g. practising drawing lines, circles and cross-hatching patterns, etc. All five children with communication difficulties will benefit from collaborative brainstorming in mixed ability groups initially, through to working closely with an adult in developing their skills in making evaluative comment in relation to the purpose of the product.

Effective learning of design and technology

Recent inspections highlight the necessity for teachers to plan design and technology activities that are progressively more demanding (OFSTED 1998). Standards of achievement have continued to improve since design and technology became part of the primary school curriculum. Teachers that demonstrate the best practice have precise learning outcomes for their pupils expressed in their planning, and they ensure that the objectives are progressively more demanding. Generic skills of designing and making ought to be advanced by each project that children undertake, and not just repeated at the same level with different materials. OFSTED suggest keeping a collection of work demonstrating processes and products as a resource for agreeing expectations within the school. Effective teaching also includes the monitoring of children's experiences and assessing their future needs.

When design and technology first became a primary school subject there was a focus on the process and children gained credit for their ingenuity in making use of materials and in solving problems. Gradually the focus became subject knowledge orientated, and schools have schemes to cover all possible aspects of the subject. The focus is now on effectiveness, and whether teachers have high enough expectations of the children.

Throughout this book, issues arise and suggestions for improving the teaching of design and technology are evident. The Activities presented have the sole aim of improving practice. It is useful to reflect and identify the essential attributes of the effective teacher in design and technology evident in each chapter:

- setting appropriately challenging tasks;
- having high expectations that all children will make progress;
- ensuring pupils combine their knowledge and understanding with their designing and making skills;

- planning for balance between designing, making and evaluating to ensure quality products;
- knowing when to intervene, and when to allow pupils to find their own solutions;
- knowing when to use focused tasks and when to use open-ended tasks;
- planning for progression in materials, tools and techniques;
- encouraging pupil evaluation of their own work;
- the ability to assess constructively and use assessments to set challenging targets.

Many teachers gauge their success by the children's response to activities. To decide whether a classroom is effective then one may look for the following features:

- Do the children understand what they are doing?
- Do they find the tasks demanding, but achievable?
- Do they willingly ask for advice?
- Do they stay on task and remain well motivated?
- Do they learn something new each lesson?

Individual progression is fundamental to the learning situation and the purpose of this book is to emphasise the issues and to create thought about how best to proceed. It does not claim to provide all the answers but hopes to spark interest in developing sound planning and assessment procedures. These procedures must involve the child, for it is the individual child for whom the teacher makes provision. The individual child is the one who makes progress or not, depending upon the provision made for the whole. Any expectations we have for our children must take notice of individual differences. The expectations for all should be high, but may not necessarily be the same for all at the same point in time. The target setting approach enables teachers to share such expectations with individual children, or groups. It provides clear assessment opportunities and records with the minimum of fuss. It gives clarity to the planning process and provides for different levels of challenge.

The whole purpose of the book is to have a clear focus on the issues. There are no apologies for using relatively simple tasks as examples, because it is by looking at simple cases that one is able to explore the complex. There are no apologies for failing to cover all aspects of the design and technology curriculum, but instead focusing on a few chosen for their unique possibilities. The focus is deliberately on the individual child, and the nature of progression from a classroom point of view, and not on the provision of a broader overview. There are no apologies for the level of demand in the activities. It is only by examining our own practice closely that we become more effective. The hope is that, on reading the book and in using the activities, the reader will gain clearer insights into the nature of progression and some ideas of how to implement practice that enables rather than inhibits. A more effective teacher of design and technology is the desired result.

Bibliography

Anning, A. (1993) 'Learning design and technology in primary schools', in McCormick, R. *et al.* (eds) *Teaching and Learning Technology.* Milton Keynes: Open University Press.

Assessment of Performance Unit (APU) (1991) *The Assessment of Performance in Design and Technology.* London: Schools Examination and Assessment Council.

Assessment of Performance Unit (APU) (1994) 'Learning through design and technology', in Banks, F. (ed.) *Teaching Technology.* London: Routledge/Open University Press.

Bell, P. (1996) *Design and Make Puppets Using Textiles.* Preston: Topical Resources.

Bennett, R. (1996) 'An investigation into some Key Stage 2 children's learning of foundation concepts associated with geared mechanisms', *Journal of Design and Technology Education* **1**(3), 218–29.

Bottrill, P. (1994) 'Textile materials for Key Stages 1 and 2: some ideas for teachers', *PrimaryDATA* **3**(3), 14–17.

Bowen, R. (1995) 'Why ask children to look at products?', *Primary DATA* **4**(2), 24–6.

Bratt, F. and Djora, J. (1995) 'Developing design and technology capability through the process diary', *PrimaryDATA* **4**(3), 9–15.

Chalkley, C. and Shield, G. (1996) 'Supermodelling! Developing designing skills at Key Stage 2', *Journal of Design and Technology Education* **1**(1), 50–53.

Constable, H. (1994a) 'The role of drawing within designing and making – a primary perspective', *PrimaryDATA* **3**(2), 8–13.

Constable, H. (1994b) 'Back to the drawing board', *Junior Education*, October, 32–3.

Constable, H. (1994c) 'How do children evaluate?', *PrimaryDATA* **3**(3), 18–23.

Curriculum Council for Wales (CCW) (1994) '"One in five": design and technology and pupils with special educational needs', in Banks, F. *Teaching Technology.* London: Routledge/Open University Press.

Dawes, A. (1996) *Design and Make Pop-up Cards for Every Occasion.* Preston: Topical Resources.

Department for Education (DfE) (1995) *Design and Technology in the National Curriculum.* London: HMSO.

Design and Technology Association (DATA) (1995a) *Design and Technology – a Pupil's Entitlement to IT at Key Stages 1 and 2.* DATA, MAPE, NAAIDT and NCET joint leaflet.

Design and Technology Association (DATA) (1995b) *Guidance Materials for Design and Technology, Key Stages 1 and 2.* London: Department for Education (DfE).

Design and Technology Association (DATA) (1995c) 'Design and technology in the nursery'. Conference presentation, DATA Annual Conference, Gloucester (not published).

Design and Technology Association (DATA) (1996a) *Guidance for Primary Phase Initial Teacher Training and Continuing Professional Development in Design and Technology – Competences for Newly Qualified and Practising Teachers.* Research Paper **7**. Wellesbourne: DATA.

Design and Technology Association (DATA) (1996b) *The Design and Technology Primary Co-ordinator's File.* Wellesbourne: DATA.

Doherty, P. *et al.* (1994) 'Planning for capability and progression for design and technology in the national curriculum', in Banks, F. (1994) *Teaching Technology.* London: Routledge/Open University Press.

Dunn, S. and Larson, R. (1990) *Design Technology – Children's Engineering.* Lewes: Falmer Press.

Gardner, D. (1995) '2D or not 2D – helping reception pupils to draw plans', *PrimaryDATA* **4**(3), 25–8.

Garvey, J. (1995) 'Drawing upon products and construction kits', *PrimaryDATA* **4**(4), 14–19.

Hardcastle, A. (1994) *Start Weaving – a Program for Introducing Weaving into Primary Schools.* Chesterfield: Technology Teaching Systems.

Hughes, M. (ed.) (1996) *Progression in Learning.* Avon: Multilingual Matters.

Johnsey, R. (1994) 'Research in primary design and technology', *PrimaryDATA* **3**(2), 25–6.

Johnsey, R. (1997) 'Improving children's performance in the procedures of design and technology', *Journal of Design and Technology* **2**(3), 201–7.

Kimbell, R. *et al.* (1995) 'D and T from 5 to 16 – a continuous experience?', *Design and Technology Teaching* **28**(1), 32–6.

Kimbell, R. *et al.* (1996) *Understanding Practice in Design and Technology.* Milton Keynes: Open University Press.

Lever, C. (1990) *National Curriculum Design and Technology for Key Stages 1, 2 and 3.* London: Trentham Books.

McCormick, R. and Davidson, M. (1996) 'Problem solving and the tyranny of product outcomes', *Journal of Design and Technology Education* **1**(3), 230–41.

Meggison, S. (1993) *Developing Role Play.* Rotherham Advisory Service, Rotherham, Yorks.

Millar, A. *et al.* (1996) 'Children's performance of investigative tasks in science: a framework for considering progression', in Hughes, M. (ed.) *Progression in Learning.* Avon: Multilingual Matters.

Munn, P. (1996) 'Progression in learning literacy and numeracy in the pre-school', in Hughes, M. (ed.) *Progression in Learning.* Avon: Multilingual Matters.

Murray, J. (1994) 'The relationship between "modelling" and designing and making with food as a material in design and technology', in Banks, F. *Teaching Technology.* London: Routledge/Open University Press.

National Association of Advisers and Inspectors in Design and Technology (NAAIDT) (1998) *Quality Through Progression.* Wellesbourne: NAAIDT Publications.

National Association of Teachers of Home Economics (NATHE) (1994) *Design and Technology Key Stages 1 and 2: Food – Details and Examples.* Leaflet. NATHE.

National Curriculum Council (NCC) (1990) *Non-Statutory Guidance. Design and Technology Capability.* York: NCC.

National Curriculum Council (NCC) (1991) *Implementing Design and Technology at Key Stages 1 and 2.* York: NCC.

Office for Standards in Education/ Department for Education (OFSTED/DfEE) (1996) *Characteristics of Good Practice in Food Technology – Key Stages 1 to 4.* London: HMSO.

Office for Standards in Education (OFSTED) (1998) *Standards in Primary Design and Technology.* Leaflet. London: OFSTED Publications.

Ritchie, R. (1995) *Primary Design and Technology – a Process for Learning.* London: David Fulton Publishers.

Schools Curriculum and Assessment Authority (SCAA) (1995a) *Design and Technology: the New Requirements, Key Stages 1 and 2.* London: SCAA.

School Curriculum and Assessment Authority (SCAA) (1995b) *Information Technology: the New Requirements, Key Stages 1 and 2.* London: SCAA.

School Curriculum and Assessment Authority (SCAA) (1995c) *Planning the Curriculum at Key Stages 1 and 2.* London: SCAA.

School Curriculum and Assessment Authority (SCAA) (1996) *Desirable Outcomes for Children's Learning on Entering Compulsory Schooling.* London: DfEE.

School Curriculum and Assessment Authority (SCAA) (1997) *Expectations in Design and Technology at Key Stages 1 and 2.* London: SCAA.

Scrine, R. and Clewes, E. (1989) *First Technology.* London: Hodder & Stoughton.

Stein, G. and Poole, P. (1997) *Design and Technology – a Primary Teacher's Handbook.* Dunstable: Folens.

Teacher Training Agency (TTA) (1998) *Assessing Your Needs in Design and Technology – Diagnostic Tasks.* London: TTA.

Teacher Training Agency (TTA) (1998) *Assessing Your Needs in Design and Technology – Diagnostic Feedback.* London: TTA.

Thompson, E. (1990) 'Promoting individuality and originality' in Tickle, L. (ed.) *Design and Technology in Primary School Classrooms.* London: Falmer Press.

VALIDATE (1996) *Design and Technology Association [DATA] Guidance Notes 3.1 – Exploring Value Judgements in Design and Technology.*

Index